Qualitative Nouns in the Pauline Epistles and Their Translation in the Revised Version

Qualitative Nouns in the Pauline Epistles and Their Translation in the Revised Version

By
ARTHUR WAKEFIELD SLATEN, PH.D.

WIPF & STOCK · Eugene, Oregon

Wipf and Stock Publishers
199 W 8th Ave, Suite 3
Eugene, OR 97401

Qualitative Nouns in the Pauline Epistles and Their Translation
in the Revised Edition
By Slaten, Arthur Wakefield
ISBN 13: 978-1-60608-753-4
Publication date 6/1/2009
Previously published by University of Chicago Press, 1918

PREFACE

The qualitative use of nouns is a subject not generally familiar, but one which, in the interests of accurate exegesis, students of the Greek New Testament cannot rightly ignore. Investigation indicates that it has been largely overlooked by both grammarians and commentators. It is hoped that the present treatment, confined necessarily to a limited field, may both serve to call attention to an important and neglected topic and lead to the application of the principles therein set forth by workers not only in other parts of the New Testament but also in the wider field of general Greek literature.

A list of the nouns used qualitatively in the Pauline Epistles is presented, showing about nine hundred nouns to be so used. Of these, fifteen have been selected for detailed study, the findings in each case being shown in the form of a statistical and comparative statement of usage, an exhibit of the usage in prepositional phrases, a discussion of the qualitative usage other than in prepositional phrases, and a consideration of the renderings of the Revised Version. The nouns thus studied are νόμος, ἁμαρτία, πίστις, δικαιοσύνη, ἐλπίς, εὐαγγέλιον, θέλημα, ἅγιος, ἀδελφός, κλητός, ἀπόστολος, ἐπίσκοπος, σωτήρ, κύριος, and θεός.

To Professor Ernest DeWitt Burton, Head of the Department of New Testament and Early Christian Literature in the University of Chicago, grateful acknowledgment is made both for the original impetus toward the investigation and for continued encouragement and helpful suggestion and criticism.

ARTHUR WAKEFIELD SLATEN

CONTENTS

PAGE

I. PROLEGOMENA 1

   1. Justification of the Present Study 1

   2. Translational Possibilities 4

      A. Variety of Possible Readings 4

      B. Comparison of Greek and English Usage 4

      C. Varieties of Error in Translation 5

   3. Scope of the Present Investigation 6

   4. The Determinative Principle in the Identification of Qualitative
      Nouns 6

   5. Translational Statistics 10

II. LIST OF THE QUALITATIVE NOUNS IN THE PAULINE EPISTLES . . 12

III. DETAILED STUDY OF SELECTED QUALITATIVE NOUNS 35
    Νόμος, 35; Ἁμαρτία, 40; Πίστις 44; Δικαιοσύνη, 47; Ἐλπίς, 49;
    Εὐαγγέλιον, 51; Θέλημα, 52; Ἅγιος, 54; Ἀδελφός, 55; Κλητός, 57;
    Ἀπόστολος, 58; Ἐπίσκοπος, 59; Σωτήρ 60; Κύριος, 62; Θεός, 64

IV. SUMMARY OF THE RESULTS OF THE STUDY 69

I. PROLEGOMENA

1. JUSTIFICATION OF THE PRESENT STUDY

On page 23 of his *Notes on New Testament Grammar* (Chicago, 1904), under the heading "Syntax of the Article," Professor Ernest D. Burton says:

"*a*) The article is in general either (1) Restrictive (demonstrative) or (2) Generic.

"*b*) Nouns without the article are either (1) Indefinite or (2) Qualitative (adjectival)."

Inasmuch as the foregoing classification of anarthrous nouns introduces a distinction recognized, so far as known, by no previous writer upon the subject, it is interesting to find Professor James Hope Moulton saying on page 83 of the Prolegomena,[1] "For exegesis there are few of the finer points of Greek which need more constant attention than this omission of the article when the writer would lay stress on the quality or character of the object. Even the Revised Version misses this badly sometimes, as in John 6:68."

These two remarks furnish the suggestion for such an investigation as the one here attempted, the first outlining the principles upon which it should proceed, the second providing it with an adequate practical object. In the course of the investigation, however, attention has necessarily been given to the classification of all nouns in the Pauline Epistles as a prerequisite to the closer study of the special selected group of nouns used qualitatively. In each case the rendering of the Revised Version has been observed and recorded. That such an intensive study of the usage of qualitative nouns is not a work of supererogation is witnessed by the fact that none of the New Testament grammars treats it in any detail.

James Hope Moulton, in the work above referred to, page 82, has a few lines on the topic "Qualitative Force in Anarthrous Nouns," merely remarking that "the lists of words which specially affect the dropped article will, of course, need careful examination for the individual cases. Thus, when Winer includes πατήρ in his list, and quotes John 1:14 and Heb. 12:7, we must feel that in both passages the

---

[1] *A Grammar of New Testament Greek*, by James Hope Moulton (3d ed.; Edinburgh, 1908), Vol. I, Prolegomena.

qualitative force is very apparent—'what son is there whom his father, *as a father*, does not chasten?' (On the former passage see R.V. margin, and the note in Winer-Moulton, p. 151)." He then adds the remark quoted at the beginning of this thesis.

A. T. Robertson in his *Short Grammar of the Greek New Testament* ([New York, 1909], p. 72) has a paragraph entitled "When the Article Is Not Used." He makes no mention of a qualitative use of nouns of which the absence of the article is an indication. In his larger work, *A Grammar of the Greek New Testament in the Light of Historical Research* ([New York, 1914], pp. 790-96), Professor Robertson discusses "The Absence of the Article." He refers to Moulton's remark above alluded to and quotes as follows: "'Few of the finer points of Greek which need more constant attention' than the absence of the article," omitting Moulton's words about the qualitative force of such cases. On page 794 Professor Robertson, discussing the absence of the article with abstract nouns, says, "No vital difference was felt between articular and anarthrous abstract nouns," citing Gildersleeve (*Syntax*, p. 259). In treating briefly of the qualitative force of nouns Professor Robertson says on the same page, "This is best brought out in anarthrous nouns," and cites a few instances.

Friedrich Blass's *Grammatik des neutestamentlichen Griechisch* (vierte, neugearbeitete Auflage, besorgt von Albert Debrunner [Göttingen, 1913], pp. 145–62), in the discussion of the article, does not mention the qualitative usage.

Gildersleeve-Miller (*Syntax of Classical Greek from Homer to Demosthenes*, Part II [New York, Cincinnati, Chicago, 1911], p. 259) says that no vital difference was felt between articular and anarthrous abstract nouns; that prepositional phrases and other formulas may dispense with the article, so also proverbs, the ordinals in expressions of time, enumerations, and βασιλεύς, of the Persian king.

Raphael Kühner (*Ausführliche Grammatik der griechischen Sprache* [Hannover und Leipzig, 1898], I, 598–610) discusses the omission of the article, listing thirteen cases, e.g., before proper names, in prepositional phrases, before abstract nouns, etc. He makes no mention of the qualitative usage, nor does he discover any principle governing the omission of the article, but merely lists various cases in which the article is omitted.

Alexander Buttmann (*A Grammar of the New Testament Greek*, English translation by J. H. Thayer [Andover, 1891]) makes no mention of the qualitative usage.

Winer-Thayer (*A Grammar of the Idiom of the New Testament* [Andover, 1874]) makes no mention of the qualitative usage of nouns.[1]

Thomas Sheldon Green (*A Treatise on the Grammar of the New Testament* [London, 1842], pp. 182–83), discussing the use of the article, recognizes the qualitative turn given in certain cases by the omission of the article. His words are as follows:

The above-mentioned omissions of the article before nouns where its presence is legitimate are only permissive; it remains to notice one that is designed.

It has already been remarked in the last section that the presence of the article is an impediment to the inherent significance of the word to which it is prefixed having a prominence or point in the sentence. Accordingly the instances which will now be brought forward are those of words to which the article might rightly be prefixed, but where it is withheld for this particular reason.

Heb. 1:1: ἐλάλησεν ἡμῖν ἐν υἱῷ.

The absence of the article may be referred to a cause just mentioned, namely, the preposition, but it is more probably intentional. Had the writer said ἐν τῷ υἱῷ the words would merely have called to mind the person already familiarly known under the title of the Son of God, without calling attention to the inherent meaning of the title; but his special concern is with his nature and attributes, namely, a design of impressing upon his readers his divine sonship, and, which is the leading idea of the epistle, his immeasurable superiority in virtue of it to all preceding persons having a divine commission. It may sound strange, but the rendering should probably be "by a Son" or "by one who is his Son," implying that God no longer addressed them by a prophet, a mere οἰκέτης, but by one who had the nature and dignity of a son. There is the same contrast in 7:28.

Summary.—In their treatment of the article grammarians have been forced to consider its frequent omission or, as Professor Robertson prefers to say, "absence." They have noted its non-appearance in various instances and have listed these. Among the cases in which the article may be omitted Green, in 1842, mentions the intentional omission of the article in order that the inherent signification of the noun may without impediment emerge. This view, which is another name for the qualitative usage, he puts forward with diffidence and caution. The

[1] Note Winer's claim in Stuart and Robinson's translation of his work entitled *A Greek Grammar of the Greek New Testament* (Andover, 1825), p. 55, that the insertion or omission of the article is a mark of individual style, and his agreement with Gersdorf (1816) that the four evangelists always write ὁ χριστός, but Paul and Peter usually χριστός, "as this appellation had in their time become a proper name."

German grammars do not recognize the qualitative usage. The English and American works of Moulton and Robertson recognize that anarthrous nouns may express a qualitative idea, but offer no thoroughgoing doctrine of the article which sets forth a definite principle governing its presence or absence. This is apparently for the first time attempted in Professor Burton's *Notes on New Testament Grammar*, referred to on page 1 of this thesis.[1]

2. TRANSLATIONAL POSSIBILITIES

A. VARIETY OF POSSIBLE READINGS

Considered purely as a matter of linguistic possibility and without regard to the correctness or incorrectness of the translation, it is obvious that in the translation of the New Testament, as of any other Greek document, into English there are the following six possibilities of rendering, viz., a Greek noun with the definite article may be rendered by: (1) an English noun with the definite article, (2) an English noun with the indefinite article, (3) an anarthrous English noun. An anarthrous Greek noun may be rendered by: (1) an anarthrous English noun, (2) an English noun with the indefinite article, (3) an English noun with the definite article. Examination shows that each of these renderings does actually occur, though naturally with varying frequency. For example, the rendering of a Greek noun with the definite article by an English noun with the indefinite article is very rare, while the rendering of an anarthrous Greek noun by an English noun with the definite article is also relatively infrequent.

B. COMPARISON OF GREEK AND ENGLISH USAGE

The observation of such phenomena is, however, but the necessary preliminary to the real task of comparison and criticism. It would be remarkable if the genius of two languages should so perfectly agree that in every case the articular usage of the one could be represented by an exactly identical idiom in the other. In the case of Greek and English such a mechanical reproduction is manifestly impossible. While in general the usage of the article in the two languages is similar and the classification quoted in the beginning obtains in both, there are certain constructions with the definite article in Greek which cannot

---

[1] The school grammars of Goodwin and of Hadley and Allen make no mention of the qualitative usage of nouns.

be rendered intelligibly in English by its employment.[1] On the other hand the indefiniteness of anarthrous Greek nouns in the singular can be expressed in English only by the prefixing of *a* or *an*.

It should be observed, however, that the prefixing of the indefinite article in English does not always result in making the noun indefinite. That qualitative character which is in Greek denoted by the absence of the article is in English frequently expressed by the employment of the indefinite article. In many instances English requires its presence, an anarthrous rendering being inadequate or awkward. Thus in the sentence "A man's a man for a' that," though the form of the nouns is identical the first is indefinite, the second qualitative. On the other hand the prefixing of *a* or *an* is not always necessary. For example, in the sentence "This can never happen while God is God and man is man," the second "God" and "man" are each qualitative, although both are anarthrous. There appears to be no rule by which one can decide in advance when the qualitative force will properly be expressed by a noun with *a* or *an* and when anarthrously. It is wholly a matter of English *Sprachgefühl*, and while to a foreigner the two forms might on occasion appear of equal desirability the trained English ear chooses infallibly between them. It is evident from these considerations that in the translation of the Greek New Testament into English a considerable divergence from Greek usage is to be expected, and the limits of such divergence will be the necessities of the case.

C. VARIETIES OF ERROR IN TRANSLATION

Translation being itself obviously a task of interpretation, the translator faces the double duty of discovering his author's meaning in Greek and of expressing that meaning adequately in English. This twofold task naturally involves a corresponding twofold liability to error. The possibilities of error in respect to the article, when carried out to their fullest form, may be enumerated as follows:

1. A translator may fail to grasp the significance of the presence or absence of the Greek article, but express that significance properly in English. In such a case error[2] could not be detected.

---

[1] Instance the infinitive with the article, nouns with the article and a following pronominal genitive, etc.

[2] The term "error" is used throughout to denote any inadequacy in translation, any failure fully to express the thought conveyed by the presence or absence of the Greek article.

2. He may fail to grasp the significance of the presence or absence of the Greek article and may fail to express that significance properly in his English translation. In this case the error is detectable.

3. He may grasp the significance of the presence or absence of the Greek article but fail to express that significance appropriately in English. In this case the error is detectable.

4. He may grasp the significance of the presence or absence of the Greek article and may properly express that significance in English. In this case there is no error.

3. SCOPE OF THE PRESENT INVESTIGATION

It is the second and the third of these possibilities that justify such an investigation as the one here attempted. In practice the two merge into one, viz., the possibility of a translator's failing adequately to express in English the significance of the presence or absence of the article in Greek. In the present study this field of possibility is still further limited to the consideration of anarthrous nouns alone, and of these to the qualitative division only, and of these again especially to those the adequacy of whose translation in the Revised Version may justly be challenged. Having classified all Greek nouns occurring in the Pauline Epistles, and having appraised their English renderings in the Revised Version, we have limited the field first by the selection of a single type, secondly by selecting from that type a special variety, and thirdly by selecting from that variety a specific class.

4. THE DETERMINATIVE PRINCIPLE IN THE IDENTIFICATION OF QUALITATIVE NOUNS

Before entering upon a discussion of such a selection of the more outstanding and characteristic Pauline terms as falls within the scope of this thesis to examine, or before enumerating the statistics pertaining to the various classes and usages of nouns which the study has discovered, it is proper at this point to insert a statement of the principle which has been determinative in the identification of qualitative nouns in this investigation and which may guide one in ascertaining whether any given anarthrous Greek noun in any Greek document is or is not qualitative. This principle may best be precisely summarized in the form of a definition. A qualitative noun is a noun (in Greek always anarthrous) whose function in the sentence is not primarily or solely to designate by assignment to a class but to describe by the attribution of quality, i.e., of the quality or qualities that are the marks of the class designated by the noun. The effect is to ascribe to that which is modified the characteristics or qualities of a class and not merely to ascribe to it membership in that class. It is the connotive rather than the denotive sense that emerges. In the sentence "Frederick is a prince" the word "prince" is either designative, marking Frederick as a member of a class, a son of a monarch, or qualitative, describing Frederick as the possessor of the superior character presumed to distinguish the son of a king. At the same time it is to be noted that the literal sense may obtain alongside the qualitative. Frederick may, for example, in fact be a prince and to him may be attributed the virtues that are regarded as proper to his station. In most instances this is precisely the design of the qualitative usage, viz., to direct the attention of the hearer or reader to the qualities or characteristics that properly belong to that which the noun designates. Each common noun designates any or all members of a class, the class being defined by the possession of certain attributes; therefore to predicate the noun of an individual, strictly speaking, both assigns it to the class and ascribes to it the attributes which distinguish the class. But in actual usage this strictness is not always maintained. Four cases may arise, viz.:

a) The individual may be assigned to the class without stress being laid upon the qualities of the class, though in fact the individual may possess them all. The noun is indefinite, e.g., Henry is a soldier.

b) Because in this case there is not much stress laid upon the qualities, the individual may be assigned to the class, though he may not possess all the qualities: Henry is a soldier (that is, a member of a military organization, though he lacks some of the soldierly qualities).

c) The qualities may be assigned to a member of the class without particular thought of the class, e.g., Henry is a soldier (i.e., has all the qualities of a soldier).

d) Because membership in the class may be little thought of, the qualities, or rather a part of them, may be ascribed to one who is not strictly a member of the class, e.g., Henry is a soldier (i.e., has soldierly qualities, though not a member of any military organization).

If one distinguish between external, formal qualities and internal qualities, in most of the cases falling under *b*) it would be the internal qualities that would be neglected, while in *d*) it is the external qualities that are forgotten. The term "soldier" denotes strictly a man who belongs to a military organization and has soldierly qualities, such as courage, etc. But we may assign him to the class, though he possess only the external qualities, or we may describe him as qualitatively a soldier, though he has only the internal qualities.   In other cases the distinction is perhaps between the proper (i.e., strict) sense of the term and its tropical sense.   In these cases the indefinite use arises when the individual possesses the qualities expressed by the term in its proper sense but is in thought assigned to the class without thought of the qualities; the qualitative use arises when emphasis is placed either upon the proper or the tropical qualities.   The great majority of the indefinite cases fall under a); the great majority of the qualitative cases fall under c).

This nuance of characteristic is usually accompanied in English by the prefixing of the indefinite article and is accomplished by an inflection of the voice.   In Greek the same effect is produced by the omission of the article and doubtless as in English (the context making clear to the reader or hearer which of the two meanings was intended) was accompanied by an appropriate vocal emphasis.   Naturally not all instances are as easily recognized as that in the illustration cited, though some are perfectly obvious, but a careful scrutiny reveals even to an English eye or ear that qualitative emphasis which the omission of the article produced for the original writer and readers.

Strictly abstract nouns, being themselves the names of qualities, are essentially qualitative, and the omission of the article serves merely to strengthen this innate qualitative force.

Appellatives are probably in their inception essentially qualitative, though they tend to become conventional titles, dropping their qualitative character.   Master and Mr. in English and *Herr* in German exemplify this fading of qualitative color.   The same process is illustrated in the word κύριος, which in modern Greek has become merely the polite Mr. or sir,[1] while in the New Testament κύριος and θεός are among those most frequently used in the qualitative sense, as a glance at the list of nouns used qualitatively will show.   In English, appellatives, whether anarthrous or preceded by the definite article, may be qualitatively used. Instance "Charles the Hammer," "Old Hickory," "Stonewall Jackson."

Proper names may also be used qualitatively, and though few instances occur in the New Testament they are not infrequently so used both in Greek and English authors.

Gentilic nouns, which are related both to appellatives and proper nouns, are occasionally used qualitatively.   A convincing example is the

---

[1] A similar usage of κύριος is apparent in the New Testament (e.g., Matt. 17:15; 18:21; 21:39; 27:63; Mark 7:28), but a return to or an emphasis upon the essential, qualitative character of the appellative is possible, so that the affirmation "Jesus is κύριος" came to be, to Paul at least, the distinctively Christian confession.

use of 'Ιουδαῖος in Rom. 2:17, where to bring out the qualitative force we might read and punctuate, "But if thou bearest the name 'Jew.'"

Common or concrete nouns both in English and Greek readily lend themselves to qualitative emphasis. Such English common nouns as "the pen," "the sword," "the scepter," "the crown," are illustrations of common nouns used qualitatively. But as a rule the definite article occurs with nouns used qualitatively only with concrete nouns used by metonymy for abstract or actional nouns. Thus "The pen is mightier than the sword" really means "Writing is more powerful than fighting." It would perhaps be strictly correct to say that a concrete generic noun is used by metonymy for a qualitative abstract or actional noun.

Though for the sake of brevity we may speak of nouns as qualitative, it is to be kept in mind that the classification is not one of nature but of usage. There is no class of qualitative nouns as such, as there is of proper, concrete, etc. Nouns of any class may be used qualitatively while retaining their natural classification. The peculiarity of qualitative usage is that the noun is so used as to lay emphasis upon the qualities or characteristics which properly belong to that which the noun represents. This qualitative emphasis does not, however, in all cases obliterate the definite reference of the noun. When the reference is commonly limited to a single person or thing, for example, the definiteness of the noun is not dissipated by the qualitative emphasis, though to express this emphasis the noun is made anarthrous. In Rom. 1:1, for example, εὐαγγέλιον, though anarthrous and qualitative, is also definite, there being but one "gospel" present to the author's mind, and the translation as will be pointed out later should run "separated unto divine good news," or "separated unto a gospel of God," the presence of the indefinite article in English not making the noun itself indefinite but expressing its qualitative character. Θεός also as commonly used in the New Testament has a distinct and limited reference to the one God, and when it is used qualitatively it does not thereby cease to be definite.

The recognition of the qualitative usage of nouns is of extreme importance in the translation and interpretation of the New Testament. That the significance of this usage is not generally recognized is apparent not only in many of the renderings of the Revised Version but even in critical commentaries upon the Greek text and in the standard grammars of New Testament Greek. While the present study of the subject maintains a constant critical surveillance of the renderings of the Revised Version as a parallel investigation, the whole is based upon the examination of New Testament Greek usage as such, and the purpose of the thesis is to aid in correct interpretation through the recognition on the part of the interpreter of this factor hitherto too much neglected, and not merely the negative task of pointing out imperfections in the current English translation.   Though the nature of the study brings into special prominence the points at which the Revised Version's neglect of the qualitative usage of nouns is most patent and its consequences most disastrous, the general merit of the translation is fully conceded.   See page 69.

5. TRANSLATIONAL STATISTICS

Preceding the detailed study of such individual qualitative nouns as it lies within the scope of the present thesis to exhibit, a statistical statement of the data discovered is appropriate.

In the Pauline Epistles (Pastorals included) there occur 8,841 nouns and noun equivalents.[1]   Classified according to their use as restrictive, generic, indefinite, and qualitative they yield the following figures: restrictive, 3,743 cases;[2] generic, 929; indefinite, 589; qualitative, 2,857.

The variety of possible translations in any given case has already been adverted to.   The findings of the present investigation are that nouns preceded by the definite article were translated:

1. By an English noun preceded by the definite article in 1,702 cases.
2. By an English noun preceded by the indefinite article in 16 cases.
3. By an anarthrous English noun in 2,954 cases.

Anarthrous Greek nouns were translated:

1. By an anarthrous English noun in 2,404 cases.
2. By an English noun preceded by the indefinite article in 397 cases.
3. By an English noun preceded by the definite article in 645 cases.

These renderings were distributed as follows:

The 3,743 restrictive nouns were rendered by English nouns preceded by the definite article in 1,480 cases; by English nouns preceded by the indefinite article in 6 cases; by anarthrous English nouns in 2,257 cases.

The 929 generic nouns were rendered by English nouns preceded by the definite article in 222 cases; by English nouns preceded by the indefinite article in 10 cases; by anarthrous English nouns in 697 cases.

---

[1] The statement has no bearing on the extent of the Pauline vocabulary.   Often the same noun occurs many times.

[2] Besides these there are 723 cases of proper names and appellatives which have been classified as restrictive without the article.

The 589 indefinite nouns were rendered by anarthrous English nouns in 405 cases; by English nouns preceded by the indefinite article in 125 cases; by English nouns preceded by the definite article in 59 cases.

The 2,857 qualitative nouns were rendered by anarthrous English nouns in 1,999 cases; by English nouns preceded by the indefinite article in 272 cases; by English nouns preceded by the definite article in 586 cases.

II. LIST OF THE QUALITATIVE NOUNS IN THE PAULINE EPISTLES

Ἀββᾶ, Rom. 8:15; 11:1; Gal. 4:6

Ἀβραάμ, Rom. 4:2, 16

ἀγαθός, Rom. 7:18, 19; 8:28; 10:15; Gal. 6:6

ἀγαθωσύνη, Rom. 15:14; Gal. 5:23; Eph. 5:9; II Thess. 1:11

ἀγανάκτησις, II Cor. 7:11

ἀγάπη, Rom. 14:15; I Cor. 4:21; 13:1, 2, 3, 13; 16:14; II Cor. 2:8;
   6:6; Gal. 5:6, 22; Eph. 1:4; 3:17; 4:2, 15, 16; 5:1; 6:23;
   Phil. 1:16; 2:1; Col. 2:2; I Thess. 5:8, 13; I Tim. 1:5; 2:15;
   4:12; 6:11; II Tim. 1:6, 13; 2:22

ἀγαπητός, Rom. 12:19; I Cor. 10:14; II Cor. 7:1; 12:19; Phil. 2:12;
   4:1

ἄγγελος, Rom. 8:38; I Cor. 6:3; II Cor. 11:14; Gal. 1:8; 3:19; 4:14;
   I Tim. 3:16

ἁγιασμός, Rom. 6:19, 22; I Cor. 1:30; I Thess. 4:4, 7; II Thess. 2:13;
   I Tim. 2:15

ἅγιος, I Cor. 1:2; Eph. 5:3; Col. 3:12; I Tim. 5:10

ἁγιωσύνη, Rom. 1:4; II Cor. 7:1; I Thess. 3:13

ἁγιότης, II Cor. 1:12

ἁγνία, I Tim. 4:12; 5:2

ἁγνότης, II Cor. 6:5

ἀγνωσία, I Cor. 15:34

ἀγριέλαιος, Rom. 11:17

ἀγρυπνία, II Cor. 6:5; 11:27

ἀγών, Col. 2:1; I Thess. 2:2

ἀδηλότης, I Tim. 6:17

ἀδελφή, I Cor. 9:5; I Tim. 5:2

ἀδελφός, Rom. 1:13; 7:1, 4; 8:12, 29; 10:1; 11:25; 12:1; 15:14, 30;
   16:17; I Cor. 1:10, 26; 2:1; 3:1; 4:6; 5:11; 6:8; 7:24, 29; 10:1;
   11:33; 14:5, 20, 26, 39; 15:1, 31, 50, 58; 16:15; II Cor. 1:6;
   8:1; 13:11; Gal. 1:10; 3:15; 4:12, 28, 31; 5:11, 13; 6:1, 18;
   Phil. 1:12; 3:1, 17; 4:1, 8; I Thess. 2:1, 9, 14, 17; 3:7; 4:1, 11, 13;
   5:1, 4, 12, 14, 25; II Thess. 1:3; 2:1, 13; 3:1, 6, 13, 15; I Tim.
   5:1; 6:2; Philem. 7, 16, 20

ἀδικία, Rom. 1:18 (*bis*), 29; 6:13; 9:14; II Thess. 2:10; II Tim. 2:19

ἄδικος, I Cor. 6:9
ἄζυμος, I Cor. 5:8
ἀήρ, I Cor. 9:26; 14:10; I Thess. 4:17
ἀθανασία, I Cor. 15:53; I Tim. 6:16
αἰδώς, I Tim. 2:9
αἷμα, Rom. 3:15; I Cor. 15:50; Gal. 1:16; Eph. 6:12
αἴνιγμα, I Cor. 13:12
αἵρεσις, I Cor. 11:19; Gal. 5:20
αἴσθησις, Phil. 1:9
αἰσχρολογία, Col. 3:8
αἰσχρός, Eph. 5:12
αἰσχρότης, Eph. 5:4
αἰχμαλωσία, Eph. 4:8
ἀκαθαρσία, Rom. 1:24; Gal. 5:20; Eph. 4:19; 5:3; Col. 3:5; I Thess. 2:3; 4:7
ἀκάθαρτος, II Cor. 6:17
ἀκαταστασία, I Cor. 14:32; II Cor. 6:5; 12:20
ἀκοή, Rom. 10:17; I Cor. 12:7; Gal. 3:2, 5; I Thess. 2:13
ἀκροβυστία, Rom. 2:25; 3:30; 4:10 (bis), 11, 12; I Cor. 7:18; Gal. 5:6; 6:15; Eph. 2:11; Col. 3:10
ἀκρογωνίαιος, Eph. 2:20
ἀλαζών, Rom. 1:30; II Tim. 3:2
ἅλας, Col. 4:6
ἀλήθεια, Rom. 2:2; 9:1; 15:8; I Cor. 5:8; II Cor. 6:7; 7:14 (bis); 11:10; 12:6; Gal. 5:7; Eph. 4:20, 25; 5:9; 6:14; Phil. 1:18; Col. 1:6; II Thess. 2:13; I Tim. 2:4, 7 (bis); II Tim. 2:25; 3:7; Titus 1:1
ἅλυσις, Eph. 6:19
ἁμαρτία, Rom. 3:9, 20; 5:13 (bis); 6:14, 16; 7:7, 8, 13, 25; 8:3 (bis), 10; 14:23; II Cor. 5:21; Gal. 2:17; 3:22; I Tim. 5:22; II Tim. 3:7
ἁμαρτωλός, Rom. 3:7; 5:8; Gal. 2:15, 17; I Tim. 1:9, 15
ἀναγκαῖος, II Cor. 9:5
ἀνάγκη, Rom. 13:5; I Cor. 7:37; 9:16; II Cor. 6:4; 9:7; 12:10; Philem. 14
ἀνάθεμα, Rom. 9:3; I Cor. 12:3; 16:21; Gal. 1:8, 9
ἀνακαίνωσις, Titus 3:5
ἀνάστασις, Rom. 1:4; I Cor. 15:12, 13, 21; II Tim. 2:18
ἀναστροφή, I Tim. 4:12
ἀνδραποδιστής, I Tim. 1:10

ἀνδροφόνος, I Tim. 1:9

ἄνεμος, Eph. 4:14

ἄνεσις, II Cor. 2:13; 7:5; 8:13; II Thess. 1:7

ἀνήρ, I Cor. 11:7, 8 (bis), 9, 11 (bis); 13:11; II Cor. 11:2; Eph. 4:13;
    I Tim. 3:2, 12; Titus 1:6

ἄνθραξ, Rom. 12:20

ἀνθρωπάρεσκος, Eph. 6:6; Col. 3:22

ἄνθρωπος, Rom. 1:23; 2:9, 29; 3:4, 5; I Cor. 2:5, 9; 3:3, 4, 21; 9:8;
    14:2; 15:21 (bis), 33, 39; II Cor. 8:21; 12:4; Gal. 1:1, 10 (ter),
    11, 12; 2:6; 3:15 (bis); Eph. 6:7; Phil. 2:7, 8; Col. 3:23; I Thess.
    2:1, 6, 13; 4:8; I Tim. 2:5 (bis); 6:16; Titus 1:14

ἀνόητος, Rom. 1:14

ἄνοιξις, Eph. 6:19

ἀνομία, II Cor. 6:14; I Tim. 1:9; Titus 2:14

ἀνόσιος, II Tim. 1:9

ἀνταπόδομα, Rom. 11:9

ἀντικείμενος, I Cor. 16:9

ἀντίλημψις, I Cor. 12:28

ἀντίλυτρον, I Tim. 2:6

ἀνυπότακτος, I Tim. 1:9

ἀπάντησις, I Thess. 4:17

ἀπαρχή, Rom. 16:5; I Cor. 15:20, 23; 16:15

ἀπάτη, II Thess. 2:10

ἀπείθεια, Rom. 11:32

ἀπελεύθερος, I Cor. 7:22

ἀπιστία, I Tim. 1:13

ἄπιστος, I Cor. 6:6; 14:23, 24; II Cor. 6:14, 15

ἁπλότης, Rom. 12:8; II Cor. 9:11, 13; Eph. 6:5; Col. 3:22

ἀπόδειξις, I Cor. 2:4

ἀποδοχή, I Tim. 4:10

ἀποκάλυψις, Rom. 2:5; 16:25; I Cor. 14:6; II Cor. 12:1; Gal. 1:12;
    2:2; Eph. 1:17; 3:3

ἀπόλαυσις, I Tim. 6:17

ἀπολογία, II Cor. 7:11; Phil. 1:16

ἀπολύτρωσις, I Cor. 1:30; Eph. 1:14; 4:30

ἀποστολή, Rom. 1:5; Gal. 2:8

ἀπόστολος, Rom. 1:1; 11:13; I Cor. 1:1; 9:1, 2; 12:28 (bis), 29;
    15:9; II Cor. 1:1; 8:23; 11:13; Gal. 1:1; Eph. 1:1; 4:11;
    Phil. 2:25; Col. 1:1; I Thess. 2:7; I Tim. 1:1; 2:7; II Tim. 1:1,
    11; Titus 1:1

ἀποτομία, Rom. 11:22 (bis)
ἀπώλεια, Rom. 9:22; Phil. 1:28; 3:18; I Tim. 6:9
ἀρά, Rom. 3:14
ἀργύριον, I Cor. 3:12
ἀρεσκία, Col. 1:10
ἀρετή, Phil. 4:8
ἁρπαγμός, Phil. 2:6
ἅρπαξ, I Cor. 5:11; 6:10
ἀρραβών, Eph. 1:14
ἀρσενοκοίτης, I Cor. 6:9; I Tim. 1:10
ἄρσην, Rom. 1:27; Gal. 3:28
ἄρτος, I Cor. 10:17; II Cor. 9:10; II Thess. 3:7
ἀρχάγγελος, I Thess. 4:16
ἀρχή, Rom. 8:38; I Cor. 15:24; Eph. 1:21; Phil. 4:15; Col. 1:16;
    2:10; II Thess. 2:13
ἀσεβής, Rom. 5:6; I Tim. 1:9
ἀσέβεια, Rom. 1:18; 11:26; II Tim. 2:17
ἀσέλγεια, Rom. 13:13; Gal. 5:20
ἀσθένεια, I Cor. 2:3; 15:43; II Cor. 12:9, 10; 13:4; Gal. 4:13
ἄσοφος, Eph. 5:15
ἀσπίς, Rom. 3:13
ἀστήρ, I Cor. 15:41 (ter)
ἀσφάλεια, I Thess. 5:2
ἀσωτία, Eph. 5:18; Titus 1:6
ἀτιμία, Rom. 1:26; 9:21; I Cor. 11:15; 15:42; II Cor. 6:8; 11:21;
    II Tim. 2:21
ἄτομος, I Cor. 15:52
αὐτάρκεια, II Cor. 9:8; I Tim. 6:6
ἀφειδία, Col. 2:23
ἀφθαρσία, Rom. 2:7; I Cor. 15:42, 53; Eph. 6:24; II Tim. 1:10
ἀφορμή, Rom. 7:8, 11; Gal. 5:13; II Cor. 5:12; 11:12
ἀφροσύνη, II Cor. 11:1, 17, 21
ἄφρων, Rom. 2:20; I Cor. 15:36

βαθμός, I Tim. 3:13
βάθος, Rom. 8:39; 11:33; II Cor. 8:2
βάπτισμα, Eph. 4:5
βάρβαρος, Rom. 1:14; I Cor. 14:11 (bis); Col. 3:10
βάρος, II Cor. 4:17; I Thess. 2:7
βασιλεία, I Cor. 15:50; Gal. 5:21

βέβηλος, I Tim. 1:9
Βενιαμείν, Rom. 11:1; Phil. 3:5
βίβλος, Phil. 4:3
βιωτικός, I Cor. 6:3, 4
βλασφημία, Eph. 4:31; Col. 3:8; I Tim. 6:4
βλάσφημος, I Tim. 1:13; II Tim. 3:2
βρέφος, II Tim. 3:15
βρῶμα, Rom. 14:15, 20; I Cor. 3:2; 8:8, 13
βρῶσις, Rom. 14:17, 20; II Cor. 9:10; Col. 2:16

γάγγραινα, II Tim. 2:17
γάλα, I Cor. 3:2
γαστήρ, I Thess. 5:3; Titus 1:12
γενεαλογία, I Tim. 1:4; Titus 3:9
γένος, II Cor. 11:26; Phil. 3:5
γεώργιον, I Cor. 3:9
γῆ, I Cor. 8:5; 15:46; Eph. 3:15
γινώσκων, Rom. 7:1
γλῶσσα, I Cor. 12:10 (bis), 28, 30; 13:8; 14:5 (bis), 6, 13, 14, 18, 19, 23, 27, 40
γνώμη, I Cor. 7:25; II Cor. 8:10
γνῶσις, Rom. 11:33; I Cor. 8:1, 10; 12:8; 13:8; 14:6; II Cor. 6:5; 8:7
γονεύς, Rom. 1:30
γράμμα, Rom. 2:27, 29; 7:6; II Cor. 3:6, 7
γραμματεύς, I Cor. 1:20; II Tim. 3:15
γραφή, Rom. 1:3; 16:26
γυμνότης, Rom. 8:35; II Cor. 11:27
γυναικάριον, II Tim. 3:6
γυνή, I Cor. 5:1; 9:5; 11:8 (bis), 9 (bis), 11 (bis); Gal. 4:4; I Tim. 5:9

δαιμόνιον, I Cor. 10:20, 21 (bis); I Tim. 4:1
δάκρυον, II Cor. 2:4
δέησις, II Cor. 9:14; Eph. 6:18 (bis)
δειλία, II Tim. 1:6
δεξιός, Rom. 8:34; Gal. 2:9; Eph. 1:20; Col. 3:1
δέσμιος, Philem. 1, 9
δεσμός, II Tim. 2:9
διάβολος, I Tim. 3:11
διαθήκη, II Cor. 3:6; Gal. 4:24
διακονία, Rom. 12:7; I Cor. 12:5; 16:15; Eph. 4:12; I Tim. 1:12; II Tim. 4:11

διάκονος, Rom. 13:4 (bis); I Cor. 3:5; II Cor. 3:6; 6:4; 11:15, 23; Gal. 2:17; Col. 1:7; I Thess. 3:2

διάκρισις, Rom. 14:1; I Cor. 12:10

διαλογισμός, Rom. 14:1; I Tim. 2:8

διαπαρατριβή, I Tim. 6:5

διαστολή, Rom. 3:22; 10:12; I Cor. 14:7

διατροφή, I Tim. 6:8

διδασκαλία, I Tim. 5:17; II Tim. 3:16

διδάσκαλος, Rom. 2:20; I Cor. 12:28, 29; Eph. 4:11; I Tim. 2:7; II Tim. 1:11

διδαχή, Rom. 6:17; I Cor. 14:6; II Tim. 4:2

δικαιοκρισία, Rom. 2:5

δίκαιος, Rom. 3:10; 5:7; II Thess. 1:5; I Tim. 1:9

δικαιοσύνη, Rom. 1:17; 3:5, 21, 22; 4:3, 5, 6, 9, 13, 22; 5:21; 6:13, 16; 8:10; 9:30 (ter), 31; 10:4, 10; 14:17; I Cor. 1:30; II Cor. 5:21; 6:14; 11:15; Gal. 2:21; 3:6; 5:5; Eph. 4:24; 5:9; Phil. 1:10; 3:6; I Tim. 6:11; II Tim. 2:22; 3:16; Titus 3:4

δικαίωμα, Rom. 5:16

δικαίωσις, Rom. 5:18

δίκη, II Thess. 1:9

διχοστασία, Gal. 5:20

δίψος, II Cor. 11:27

διωγμός, Rom. 8:35; II Cor. 12:10; II Tim. 3:11

διώκτης, I Tim. 1:13

δόγμα, Eph. 2:15

δοκιμή, Rom. 5:3; II Cor. 8:1; 13:3

δόλος, Rom. 1:29; II Cor. 12:16; I Thess. 2:3

δόμα, Eph. 4:8

δόξα, Rom. 2:7, 10; 4:20; 9:23; 15:7; I Cor. 2:7; 10:31; 11:7 (bis), 15; 15:41 (quater), 42; II Cor. 1:20; 3:7, 8, 9 (bis), 11 (bis), 18 (bis); 4:17; 6:8; 8:23; Eph. 1:6, 12; 3:13; Phil. 1:10; 2:10; 4:19; Col. 3:4; I Thess. 2:6; II Thess. 2:14; I Tim. 1:17; 3:16; II Tim. 2:10

δόσις, Phil. 4:15

δουλεία, Rom. 8:15; Gal. 4:24; 5:1

δοῦλος, Rom. 1:1; 6:16 (bis), 17, 20; I Cor. 7:21, 22 (bis), 23; 12:13; II Cor. 4:5; Gal. 1:10; 3:28; 4:1, 7; Eph. 6:7, 8; Phil. 1:1; 2:7; Col. 3:11; 4:12; Titus 1:1; Philem. 15 (bis)

δύναμις, Rom. 1:4, 16, 20; 8:38; 15:13, 19 (bis); I Cor. 1:18, 24; 2:4, 5; 4:20; 12:9, 28, 29; 15:24, 43; II Cor. 1:8; 6:7; 8:3 (bis);

12:12; 13:4 (*bis*); Gal. 3:5; ·Eph. 1:21; 3:16; Col. 1:11, 29;
    I Thess. 1:5; II Thess. 1:7, 11; 2:9; II Tim. 1:6, 8
δυνατός, I Cor. 1:26
δυσφημία, II Cor. 6:8

Ἑβραῖος, II Cor. 11:22; Phil. 3:5 (*bis*)
ἐγκράτεια, Gal. 5:23
ἑδραίωμα, I Tim. 3:15
ἐθελοθρησκεία, Col. 2:23
ἔθνος, Rom. 2:14; 3:29 (*bis*); 9:24, 30; 11:12, 13; 15:10, 12 (*bis*), 18;
    I Cor. 1:23; 12:2; II Cor. 11:26; Gal. 2:15; I Tim. 2:7; 3:16 ·
εἶδος, II Cor. 5:7
εἰδωλόθυτος, I Cor. 8:7
εἰδωλολάτρης, I Cor. 5:11
εἰδωλολατρία, I Cor. 6:9; 10:7; Gal. 5:20; Col. 3:5
εἴδωλον, II Cor. 6:16
εἰκών, I Cor. 11:7; II Cor. 4:4; Col. 1:15; 3:10
εἰλικρίνεια, I Cor. 5:8; II Cor. 1:12; 2:17
εἰρήνη, Rom. 1:7; 2:10; 3:17; 5:1; 8:6; 14:17; 15:13; I Cor. 1:3;
    7:15; 14:33; 16:11; II Cor. 1:2; Gal. 1:3; 5:22; 6:16; Eph. 1:2;
    2:15, 17 (*bis*); 6:23; Phil. 1:2; Col. 1:2; I Thess. 1:1; 5:2;
    II Thess. 1:2; I Tim. 1:2; II Tim. 1:2; 2:22; Titus 1:4; Philem. 3
ἐκδίκησις, Rom. 12:19; II Cor. 7:11; II Thess. 1:8
ἔκδικος, Rom. 13:4; I Thess. 4:6
ἐκζήτησις, I Tim. 1:4
ἐκζητῶν, Rom. 3:11
ἐκκλησία, I Cor. 11:18; 14:5, 19, 28, 35; II Cor. 8:23; I Tim. 3:15
ἐκλεκτός, Rom. 8:33; Col. 3:11; Titus 1:1
ἐκλογή, Rom. 9:11; 11:5
ἑκούσιος, Philem. 14
ἐλεγμός, II Tim. 3:16
ἔλεος, Rom. 9:23; 15:9; Gal. 6:16; Eph. 2:4; I Tim. 1:2; II Tim.
    1:2, 16, 18
ἐλευθερία, II Cor. 3:17; Gal. 5:13
ἐλεύθερος, I Cor. 7:21, 22; 12:13; Gal. 3:28; Eph. 6:8; Col. 3:11
Ἕλλην, Rom. 1:14, 16; 2:9, 10; 3:9; 10:12; I Cor. 1:22, 24; 10:32;
    12:13; Gal. 2:4; 3:28
ἐλπίς, Rom. 4:18 (*bis*); 5:2, 4; 8:20, 24; I Cor. 9:10 (*bis*); 13:13;
    II Cor. 3:12; 10:15; Gal. 5:5; Eph. 2:12; 4:4; I Thess. 2:19;
    4:13; 5:8; II Thess. 2:16; Titus 1:1; 3:7

ἐναντίος, Titus 2:8
ἔνδειγμα, II Thess. 1:4
ἔνδειξις, Rom. 3:25; Phil. 1:28
ἐνέργεια, Eph. 4:16; II Thess. 2:9, 11
ἐνέργημα, I Cor. 12:6
ἐνεστώς, Rom. 8:38; I Cor. 3:22
ἐνιαυτός, Gal. 4:10
ἐνκοπή, I Cor. 9:12
ἔντευξις, I Tim. 4:5
ἐντολή, I Cor. 7:19; 14:38; Eph. 6:2; Titus 1:14
ἐντροπή, I Cor. 6:4; 15:34
ἐξουσία, Rom. 9:21; 13:1 (bis); I Cor. 7:37; 9:4, 5, 6; 11:10; 15:24;
    Eph. 1:21; Col. 1:16; 2:10; II Thess. 3:9
ἑορτή, Col. 2:16
ἐπαγγελία, Rom. 9:9; Gal. 3:18 (bis), 29; 4:23, 28; Eph. 6:2; I Tim.
    4:9; II Tim. 1:1
ἔπαινος, Rom. 13:3; Eph. 1:6, 12, 14; Phil. 1:10; 4:8
ἐπανόρθωσις, II Tim. 3:16
ἐπίγειος, Phil. 2:10
ἐπίγνωσις, Rom. 1:28; 3:20; 10:2; Phil. 1:9; Col. 2:2; 3:10; I Tim.
    2:4; II Tim. 2:25; 3:7; Titus 1:1; Philem. 6
ἐπίθεσις, I Tim. 4:14
ἐπιθυμητής, I Cor. 10:6
ἐπιθυμία, Rom. 7:8; 13:14; Gal. 5:16; Col. 3:5; I Thess. 2:17; 4:5;
    I Tim. 6:9; II Tim. 3:7
ἐπίορκος, I Tim. 1:10
ἐπιπόθησις, II Cor. 7:11
ἐπιποθία, Rom. 15:23
ἐπισκοπή, I Tim. 3:1
ἐπιστολή, I Cor. 16:3; II Cor. 3:3; 10:11; II Thess. 2:2, 15
ἐπιταγή, Rom. 16:26; I Cor. 7:6; II Cor. 8:8; I Tim. 1:1; Titus 1:3;
    2:15
ἐπίτροπος, Gal. 4:2
ἐπιχορηγία, Phil. 1:19
ἐπουράνιος, Phil. 2:10
ἐργασία, Eph. 4:19
ἐργάτης, II Cor. 11:13; II Tim. 2:15
ἔργον, Rom. 2:7; 3:20, 28; 4:2, 6; 9:11, 32; 10:19; 11:6; 15:18; Gal.
    2:16 (ter); 3:2, 5, 10; Eph. 2:9, 10; 4:12; Phil. 1:22; Col. 3:17;
    II Thess. 1:11; I Tim. 2:10; 6:17; II Tim. 4:5; Titus 3:5, 8, 14

ἐρημία, I Cor. 12:10; II Cor. 11:26
ἐριθία, II Cor. 12:20; Gal. 5:20; Phil. 1:16; 2:2
ἔρις, Rom. 1:29; 13:13; I Cor. 1:11; 3:3; II Cor. 12:20; Gal. 5:20; Phil. 1:15; I Tim. 6:4; Titus 3:9
ἑρπετόν, Rom. 1:23
ἔσοπτρον, I Cor. 13:12
ἑτερόγλωσσος, I Cor. 14:21
ἑτοιμασία, Eph. 6:15
ἕτοιμος, II Cor. 10:6
εὐαγγέλιον, Rom. 1:2; II Cor. 11:4; Gal. 1:6; II Thess. 2:14
εὐαγγελιστής, Eph. 4:11; II Tim. 4:5
εὐγενής, I Cor. 1:26
εὐδοκία, Phil. 1:15; II Thess. 1:11
εὐλογία, Rom. 15:29; II Cor. 9:5, 6 (bis); Eph. 1:3
εὔνοια, Eph. 6:7
εὐσέβεια, I Tim. 2:2; 4:8; 6:3; I Tim. 6:11; II Tim. 3:5; Titus 1:1
εὐσχημοσύνη, I Cor. 12:23
εὐτραπελία, Eph. 5:4
εὐφημία, II Cor. 6:8
εὐχαριστία, Col. 2:7; 4:2; I Thess. 3:9; II Cor. 9:11; Eph. 5:4; Phil. 4:6; I Tim. 4:3, 4
εὐωδία, II Cor. 2:15; Eph. 5:2; Phil. 4:18
ἐφευρετής, Rom. 1:30
ἔχθρα, Rom. 8:7; I Cor. 15:26; Gal. 5:20; II Thess. 3:15
ἐχθρός, Rom. 5:10; 11:28; Gal. 4:16; Col. 1:20

ζῆλος, Rom. 10:2; 13:13; I Cor. 3:3; II Cor. 7:11; 11:2; 12:20; Gal. 5:20; Phil. 3:6
ζηλωτής, Gal. 1:14; Titus 2:14
ζημία, Phil. 3:7, 8
ζήτησις, I Tim. 6:4; Titus 3:9
ζυγός, Gal. 5:1; I Tim. 6:1
ζύμη, I Cor. 5:8 (bis); Gal. 5:9
ζωή, Rom. 2:7; 5:18, 21; 6:4, 22, 23; 7:10; 8:6, 10, 38; 11:15; I Cor. 3:22; II Cor. 2:16 (bis); Gal. 6:8; Phil. 1:20; 2:16; 4:3; I Tim. 1:16; 4:9; II Tim. 1:1, 10; Titus 1:1; 3:7
ζῶντες, Rom. 14:9; II Tim. 4:1

ἠγαπημένος, Col. 3:12
ἡλικία, Eph. 4:13

ἥλιος, I Cor. 15:41
ἡμέρα, Rom. 2:5, 16; 13:13; I Cor. 4:3; 15:31; II Cor. 4:16 (bis);
  11:28; Gal. 4:10; Phil. 2:16; I Thess. 2:9; 3:10; 5:2, 5, 8;
  II Thess. 3:8; I Tim. 5:5; II Tim. 1:4
ἡσυχία, II Thess. 3:12; I Tim. 2:11, 12

θάλασσα, II Cor. 11:26
θάνατος, Rom. 1:32; 6:9, 16, 21, 23; 7:10, 13 (bis); 8:6, 38; I Cor. 3:22;
  15:21, 55 (bis); II Cor. 1:10; 2:16 (bis); 4:11; 7:10; 11:23;
  Phil. 1:20; 2:8, 9, 27, 30
θαῦμα, II Cor. 11:14
θέατρον, I Cor. 4:9
θειότης, Rom. 1:20
θέλημα, Rom. 15:32; I Cor. 1:1; 16:12; II Cor. 1:1; 8:5; Eph. 1:1;
  Col. 1:1; 4:12; I Thess. 4:3; 5:18; II Tim. 1:1
θεμέλιος, I Cor. 3:10; I Tim. 6:19
θεός, Rom. 1:2, 4, 17, 18, 21; 2:17; 3:5, 18, 21, 22; 4:2, 17; 7:25;
  8:7, 8, 9, 14, 16, 17, 27, 33; 9:5, 26; 10:2; 11:22 (bis); 13:1 (bis);
  15:32; I Cor. 1:1, 3, 20, 24 (bis), 30; 2:5, 6; 3:8, 9 (bis), 16;
  4:1; 7:24, 40; 8:4, 6; 10:20; 12:3; 14:2; II Cor. 6:16; 7:9, 10;
  11:2; 13:4 (bis); Gal. 4:8; Eph. 1:1; 4:6; Phil. 2:15; 3:3;
  Col. 1:1; 3:12; I Thess. 2:1, 13; 5:18; II Thess. 1:8; 2:4 (bis);
  I Tim. 1:4, 17; 2:5; 6:17; II Tim. 1:1, 8; Titus 1:1
θεοσέβεια, I Tim. 2:10
θεοστυγής, Rom. 1:30
θῆλυς, Gal. 3:28
θήρα, Rom. 11:9
θηρίον, Titus 1:12
θλίψις, Rom. 2:9; 8:35; I Cor. 7:28; II Cor. 2:4; 6:4; 7:13; 8:2, 13;
  Phil. 1:17; I Thess. 1:6; II Thess. 1:6
θρησκεία, Col. 2:18
θρόνος, Col. 1:16
θυγάτηρ, II Cor. 6:18
θυμός, Rom. 2:8; II Cor. 12:20; Gal. 5:20; Eph. 4:31; Col. 3:8
θύρα, I Cor. 16:9
θυσία, Rom. 12:1; Eph. 5:2; Phil. 4:18
θώραξ, I Thess. 5:8

ἴαμα, I Cor. 12:9, 28, 30
ἰδιώτης, I Cor. 14:23, 24; II Cor. 11:6

ἱερόθυτος, I Cor. 10:28
Ἰησοῦς, II Cor. 11:4
ἱλαρότης, Rom. 12:8
ἱλαστήριον, Rom. 3:25
ἱματισμός, I Tim. 2:9
ἰός, Rom. 3:13
Ἰουδαῖος, Rom. 1:16; 2:9, 10, 17, 28, 29; 3:9, 29; 9:24; 10:12; I Cor. 1:22, 23, 24; 9:20; 10:32; 12:13; II Cor. 11:24; Gal. 2:14, 15; 3:28; Col. 3:11
ἰσότης, II Cor. 8:14 (*bis*)
Ἰσραήλ, Rom. 9:6; Phil. 3:5
Ἰσραηλίτης, Rom. 8:4; 11:1; II Cor. 11:22
ἰχθύς, I Cor. 15:39

καθαίρεσις, II Cor. 10:4, 8; 13:10
καινότης, Rom. 6:4; 7:6
καιρός, Rom. 5:6; I Cor. 4:4; Gal. 4:10; 6:9, 10
κακία, Rom. 1:29; I Cor. 5:8; Eph. 4:31; Col. 3:8; Titus 3:3
κακοηθία, Rom. 1:29
κακός, Rom. 7:19; 12:17 (*bis*); 13:10; 14:20; I Cor. 10:6; I Thess. 5:15 (*bis*); II Tim. 4:14
κακοῦργος, II Tim. 2:9
καλάμη, I Cor. 3:12
καλλιέλαιος, Rom. 11:24
καλός, Rom. 12:17; 14:21; II Cor. 8:20; Gal. 4:18 (*bis*)
κάλυμμα, II Cor. 3:15
καρδία, Rom. 2:5, 29; 6:17; 10:10; I Cor. 2:9; II Cor. 2:4; 3:3; 5:12; Col. 3:22; I Thess. 2:17; I Tim. 1:5; II Tim. 2:22
καρπός, Rom. 6:21; Phil. 1:22
κατάκριμα, Rom. 5:16; 8:1
κατάκρισις, II Cor. 7:3
καταλαλιά, II Cor. 12:20
κατάλαλος, Rom. 1:30
καταλλαγή, Rom. 11:15
κατάνυξις, Rom. 11:8
κατάρα, Gal. 3:10, 13
κατάστημα, Titus 2:3
καταστολή, I Tim. 2:9
καταχθόνιος, Phil. 2:10
κατηγορία, Titus 1:6

κατοικητήριον, Eph. 2:22
καύχημα, Rom. 4:2; I Cor. 9:16; II Cor. 1:13; 5:12; Phil. 2:16
καύχησις, II Cor. 7:4; I Thess. 2:19
κέλευσμα, I Thess. 4:16
κενοδοξία, Phil. 2:2
κενός, Gal. 2:2; Phil. 2:16 (bis); I Thess. 3:5
κέρδος, Phil. 1:21; 3:7; Titus 1:10
κεφαλή, I Cor. 11:3 (bis), 4; Eph. 1:22; 5:23 (bis)
κήρυγμα, Titus 1:3
κῆρυξ, I Tim. 2:7; II Tim. 1:11
κίνδυνος, Rom. 8:35; II Cor. 11:26 (octies)
κλάδος, Rom. 11:19
κλαίων, Rom. 12:15
κλέπτης, I Cor. 6:10; I Thess. 5:2, 4
κληρονομία, Eph. 5:5
κληρονόμος, Rom. 4:13; 8:17 (bis); Gal. 3:29; 4:7
κλῆσις, II Tim. 1:9
κλητός, Rom. 1:6
κοιλία, Gal. 1:15
κοινωνία, I Cor. 1:9; 10:16 (bis); II Cor. 6:14; Gal. 2:9; Phil. 2:1
κοινωνός, I Cor. 10:18, 20; II Cor. 1:7; Philem. 17
κοίτη, Rom. 9:10; 13:13
κόκκος, I Cor. 15:37
κολακία, I Thess. 2:5
κόπος, II Cor. 6:5; 11:23, 27; Gal. 6:17; II Thess. 3:8
κόσμος, Rom. 1:20; 4:13; 5:13; 11:12, 15; I Cor. 3:22; 14:10; II Cor.
    5:19; Gal. 6:14; Eph. 1:4; Phil. 2:15; I Tim. 3:16
κράτος, I Tim. 6:16
κραυγή, Eph. 4:31
κρέας, Rom. 14:21; I Cor. 8:13
κρίμα, Rom. 13:2; I Cor. 11:29, 34; I Tim. 3:6; 5:12
κρίσις, I Tim. 5:24
κριτήριον, I Cor. 6:2
κτῆνος, I Cor. 15:39
κτίσις, Rom. 1:20; 8:39; II Cor. 5:17; Gal. 6:15
κυβέρνησις, I Cor. 12:28
κύκλος, Rom. 15:19
κύμβαλον, I Cor. 13:1
κύριος, Rom. 1:7; 10:9; 16:8, 11, 12 (bis), 13, 22; I Cor. 1:3; 4:17;
    7:22, 39; 8:6; 9:1, 2; 10:21 (bis); 11:11; 12:3; 15:58; 16:19;

II Cor. 2:12; 4:5; 11:17; Gal. 4:1; 5:10; Eph. 2:21; 4:1, 5, 17; 5:8; 6:10, 21; Phil. 2:10; 3:1; 4:2, 10; Col. 3:17; 4:1; I Thess. 5:12; II Thess. 3:4, 12; Philem. 16
κυριότης, Eph. 1:21; Col. 1:16
κῶμος, Rom. 13:13; Gal. 5:21

λαός, Rom. 9:25, 26; II Cor. 6:16
λάχανον, Rom. 14:2
λειτουργός, Rom. 15:16; Phil. 2:25
λέων, II Tim. 4:17
λήμψις, Phil. 3:15
λῃστής, II Cor. 11:26
λίθος, I Cor. 3:12; II Cor. 3:7
λίμμα, Rom. 11:5
λιμός, Rom. 8:35; II Cor. 11:27
λογισμός, II Cor. 10:5
λογομαχία, I Tim. 6:4
λόγος, Rom. 9:28; 14:12; 15:18; I Cor. 1:17; 2:1, 4; 4:20; 14:9; 15:2; II Cor. 6:7; 8:7; Eph. 5:6; 6:19; Phil. 2:16; 4:15, 17; Col. 2:23; 3:17; I Thess. 1:5; 2:5, 13 (ter); 4:15; II Thess. 2:2, 15; I Tim. 4:5, 12; 5:17; 6:3; II Tim. 1:13
λοιδορία, I Tim. 5:14
λοίδορος, I Cor. 5:11; 6:10
λουτρόν, Titus 3:5
λύπη, Rom. 9:2; II Cor. 2:1, 3; 9:1, 7; Phil. 2:27 (bis)
λύσις, I Cor. 7:27

μάκελλον, I Cor. 10:25
μακροθυμία, Rom. 9:22; II Cor. 6:6; Gal. 5:23; Eph. 4:2; Col. 1:11; 3:12; II Tim. 4:2
μαλακός, I Cor. 6:9
μαργαρίτης, I Tim. 2:9
μαρτυρία, I Tim. 3:7
μάρτυς, Rom. 1:9; I Cor. 15:15; II Cor. 1:23; Phil. 1:8; I Thess. 2:6, 10
ματαιολογία, I Tim. 1:6
ματαιολόγος, Titus 1:9
ματαιότης, Eph. 4:17
μάχαιρα, Rom. 8:35
μάχη, II Cor. 7:5; II Tim. 2:23; Titus 3:9
μέθη, Rom. 13:13; Gal. 5:20

μέθυσος, I Cor. 5:11; 6:10
μέλας, II Cor. 3:3
μέλλον, Rom. 8:39; I Cor. 3:22
μέλος, Rom. 12:4, 5; I Cor. 12:14, 19, 20, 27; Eph. 4:25; 5:30
μερίς, II Cor. 6:15
μέρος, Rom. 11:25; 15:15, 24; I Cor. 5:2; 11:18; 12:27; 13:9 (bis),
    10, 12; 14:27; II Cor. 1:13; 2:5; Col. 2:16
μεσίτης, Gal. 3:19; I Tim. 2:5
μέσος, II Cor. 6:17; I Thess. 2:7; II Thess. 2:8
μετάλημψις, I Tim. 4:3
μετάνοια, Rom. 2:4; II Cor. 7:9, 10; II Tim. 2:25
μετοχή, II Cor. 6:14
μέτρον, II Cor. 10:13; Eph. 4:13, 16
μήν, Gal. 4:10
μήτηρ, Gal. 1:15; 4:27; I Tim. 5:2
μητραλοίας, I Tim. 1:9
μιμητής, I Cor. 4:16; 11:1; Eph. 5:1; I Thess. 1:6; 2:14
μισθός, I Cor. 3:15; 9:17
μνεία, Eph. 1:10, 16; I Thess. 1:2; 3:6; Philem. 4
μοιχαλίς, Rom. 7:3 (bis)
μοιχός, I Cor. 6:9
μορφή, Phil. 2:5, 7
μόρφωσις, II Cor. 3:5
μόχθος, II Cor. 11:27; II Thess. 3:8
μῦθος, I Tim. 1:4; Titus 1:14
μυστήριον, Rom. 16:25; I Cor. 4:1; 14:2
μωρία, I Cor. 1:18, 23; 2:14; 3:19
μωρολογία, Eph. 5:4
μωρός, I Cor. 3:18

ναί, II Cor. 1:18, 19 (bis)
ναός, I Cor. 3:16; 6:19; II Cor. 6:16 (bis); Eph. 2:21
νεκρός, Rom. 1:4; 4:24; 6:4, 9, 13; 7:4; 8:11 (bis), 34; 10:8, 9; 11:15;
    14:9; I Cor. 15:12, 13, 15, 16, 20, 21, 29, 32; Gal. 1:1; Eph. 1:20;
    Phil. 3:11; Col. 2:12; II Tim. 2:8; 4:1
νεομηνία, Col. 2:16
νεόφυτος, I Tim. 3:6
νεφέλη, I Thess. 4:17
νήπιος, Rom. 2:20; I Cor. 3:1; 13:11 (quater); Gal. 4:1, 3; Eph. 4:14;
    I Thess. 2:7

νηστεία, II Cor. 6:5; 11:27
νῖκος, I Cor. 15:54
νομή, II Tim. 2:17
νομοδιδάσκαλος, I Tim. 1:7
νόμος, Rom. 2:12 (*bis*), 13 (*bis*), 17, 23*a*, 25 (*bis*); 3:20, 21, 28, 31 (*bis*);
     4:13, 14, 15; 5:13 (*bis*), 20; 6:14, 15; 7:1, 2, 7, 8, 9; 9:31; 10:4, 5;
     13:8, 10; I Cor. 9:20 (*quater*); Gal. 2:16 (*ter*), 19 (*bis*), 21; 3:2, 5,
     10, 11, 18, 21, 23; 4:4, 5, 21; 5:4, 19, 24; 6:13; Phil. 3:5, 6, 9;
     I Tim. 1:9
νουθεσία, I Cor. 10:11; Eph. 6:4
νοῦς, Rom. 11:34; I Cor. 2:16 (*bis*); Phil. 4:7
νύξ, I Thess. 2:9; 3:10; 5:2, 6, 7 (*bis*); II Thess. 3:8; I Tim. 5:5;
     II Tim. 1:4

ξενία, Philem. 22
ξένος, Eph. 2:12, 19
ξύλον, I Cor. 3:12; Gal. 3:13

ὁδηγός, Rom. 2:19
ὁδοιπορία, II Cor. 11:26
ὁδός, Rom. 3:17
ὀδύνη, Rom. 9:2; I Tim. 6:10
οἰκία, I Cor. 11:22
οἰκοδομή, Rom. 15:2; I Cor. 3:9; 14:3, 5, 26; II Cor. 5:1; 10:8; 13:10;
     Eph. 4:13, 16, 29
οἰκεῖος, Eph. 2:19; I Tim. 5:8
οἰκονομία, I Cor. 9:17; Eph. 1:10; I Tim. 1:4
οἰκονόμος, I Cor. 4:1; Gal. 4:2; Titus 1:7
οἶκος, Rom. 16:5; I Tim. 3:15; Titus 1:10; Philem. 2
οἰκτιρμός, Phil. 2:1; Col. 3:12
οἶνος, Rom. 14:21
ὄλεθρος, I Cor. 5:5; I Thess. 5:3; II Thess. 1:9; I Tim. 6:9
ὀλίγος, Eph. 3:3; I Tim. 4:8
ὁμιλία, I Cor. 15:33
ὁμοίωμα, Rom. 8:3; Phil. 2:7
ὀνειδισμός, I Tim. 3:7
ὄνομα, Eph. 1:21; 5:20; Col. 3:17; II Thess. 3:6
ὅπλον, Rom. 6:13 (*bis*)
ὀπτασία, II Cor. 12:1
ὀργή, Rom. 1:18; 2:5 (*bis*), 8; 9:22; 13:4; Eph. 2:3; 4:31; Col. 3:8;
     I Thess. 5:9; I Tim. 2:8

ὅρος, I Cor. 13:2
ὁσιότης, Eph. 4:24
ὀσμή, II Cor. 2:16 (bis); Eph. 5:2; Phil. 4:18
οὖ, II Cor. 1:18, 19
οὐρανός, Rom. 1:18;, I Cor. 8:5; 15:47; II Cor. 5:2; 12:2; Gal. 1:8;
    Eph. 3:15; 6:9; Phil. 3:20; Col. 4:1; II Thess. 1:7
οὖς, I Cor. 2:9
ὀφειλέτης, Rom. 1:14; 8:12; 15:27; Gal. 5:3
ὀφείλημα, Rom. 4:4
ὀφθαλμοδουλία, Eph. 6:6; Col. 3:22
ὀφθαλμός, I Cor. 2:9; 12:16 (bis); 15:52; Gal. 3:1
ὀχύρωμα, II Cor. 10:4
ὀψώνιον, I Cor. 9:6; II Cor. 11:8

παγίς, Rom. 11:9; I Tim. 6:9
πάθος, Rom. 1:26; Col. 3:5; I Thess. 4:5
παιδαγωγός, I Cor. 4:15; Gal. 3:24, 25
παιδεία, I Cor. 14:20; Eph. 6:4; II Tim. 3:16
παιδευτής, Rom. 2:20
παιδίσκη, Gal. 4:31
παλαιότης, Rom. 7:6
παλινγενεσία, Titus 3:5
πανουργία, II Cor. 4:2; Eph. 4:14
παντοκράτωρ, II Cor. 6:18
παράβασις, Rom. 4:15; I Tim. 2:14
παραβάτης, Gal. 2:18
παράκλησις, I Cor. 14:3; II Cor. 1:3; 8:4; Phil. 2:1; II Thess. 2:16;
    Philem. 7
παραμυθία, I Cor. 14:3
παραμύθιον, Phil. 2:1
παρηγορία, Col. 4:11
παρθένος, II Cor. 11:2
πάροδος, I Cor. 16:7
πάροικος, Eph. 2:19
παροργισμός, Eph. 4:26
παρρησία, II Cor. 3:12; 7:4; Eph. 6:19; Phil. 1:20; Col. 2:15; I Tim.
    3:13; Philem. 8
πατήρ, Rom. 4:11, 12, 16, 17, 18; I Cor. 1:3; 4:15; II Cor. 1:2; 6:17;
    Gal. 1:1, 3, 4; Eph. 1:2; 4:6; Phil. 1:2; 2:10, 22; Col. 1:3 (bis);
    3:17; I Thess. 1:1; 2:11; I Tim. 1:2; 5:1; II Tim. 1:2; Titus
    1:4; Philem. 3

πατραλῴας, I Tim. 1:9
πειρασμός, I Tim. 6:9
πεποίθησις, II Cor. 8:22; Eph. 3:12; Phil. 3:4
περιβόλαιον, I Cor. 11:15
περικάθαρμα, I Cor. 4:13
περικεφαλαία, I Thess. 5:8
περιποίησις, I Thess. 5:9; II Thess. 2:14
περισσεία, II Cor. 10:15
περιτομή, Rom. 2:25, 26, 27, 29; 3:30; 4:10 (bis), 11, 12; 15:8; Gal.
    2:12; 5:6, 11; 6:15; Eph. 3:5; Col. 2:11; 3:10; 4:11
περίψημα, I Cor. 4:13
πετεινός, Rom. 1:23
πιθανολογία, Col. 2:4
πικρία, Rom. 3:14; Eph. 4:31
πίστις, Rom. 1:5, 17 (ter); 3:22, 25, 27, 28, 30; 4:13, 16 (bis); 5:1;
    9:30, 32; 10:6; 12:3; 14:22, 23 (bis); 16:26; I Cor. 12:9; 13:13;
    II Cor. 5:7; 8:7; Gal. 2:16 (bis), 20; 3:2, 5, 7, 8, 9, 11, 12, 22, 24;
    5:5, 6, 23; Eph. 2:8; 4:5; 6:23; Phil. 3:9; I Thess. 5:8; II Thess.
    1:11; 2:13; I Tim. 1:1, 4, 5, 14, 19; 2:7, 15; 3:13; 4:12; 6:11;
    II Tim. 1:13; 2:22; 3:15; Titus 1:1, 4; 2:10; 3:15
πιστός, II Cor. 6:15; I Tim. 4:10
πλάνη, I Thess. 2:3; II Thess. 2:11
πλείων, II Tim. 2:16; 3:8
πλεονέκτης, I Cor. 5:11; 6:10
πλεονεξία, Rom. 1:29; II Cor. 9:5; Eph. 4:19; I Thess. 2:5
πληγή, II Cor. 6:5; 11:23
πλήκτης, Titus 1:7
πληροφορία, I Thess. 1:5
πλήρωμα, Rom. 13:10; 15:29
πλησμονή, Col. 2:23
πλοῦτος, Rom. 11:12 (bis), 33; Col. 2:2; I Tim. 6:17
πνεῦμα, Rom. 1:4; 2:29; 5:5; 7:6; 8:4, 5, 9 (ter), 13, 14; 9:1; 14:17;
    15:13, 16, 19; I Cor. 2:4, 13; 6:17; 7:40; 12:3 (bis), 13; 14:2, 16;
    15:45; II Cor. 3:3, 6, 18; 6:6; 7:1; 11:4; Gal. 3:3; 4:29; 5:5, 6,
    18, 25 (bis); Eph. 2:18, 22; 4:4; 5:18; 6:18; Phil. 1:27; 2:1;
    3:3; Col. 1:8; I Thess. 1:5, 6; II Thess. 2:2, 13; I Tim. 1:6, 14
    Titus 3:5
πνευματικός, I Cor. 2:14 (bis); 3:1; 14:37; 15:44
ποίημα, Eph. 2:10
ποιμήν, Eph. 4:11
ποιῶν, Rom. 3:12

πόλεμος, I Cor. 14:8
πόλις, II Cor. 11:26; Titus 1:5
πονηρία, Rom. 1:29; I Cor. 5:8
πόνος, Col. 4:13
πορισμός, I Tim. 6:5, 6
πορνεία, I Cor. 5:1 (bis); Gal. 5:20; Eph. 5:3; Col. 3:5
πόρνη, I Cor. 6:5
πόρνος, I Cor. 5:9, 11; 6:9; I Tim. 1:10
πόσις, Rom. 14:17; Col. 2:16
ποταμός, II Cor. 11:26
πραϋπαθία, I Tim. 6: 11
πραΰτης, I Cor. 4:21; Gal. 5:23; 6:1; Eph. 4:2; Col. 3:12; II Tim. 2:25
πρεσβύτης, Philem. 9
πρόβατον, Rom. 8:36
πρόγονος, II Tim. 1:3
πρόθεσις, Rom. 8:28; Eph. 1:11; 3:11; II Tim. 1:9
προκοπή, Phil. 1:12
πρόκριμα, I Tim. 5:21
πρόνοια, Rom. 13:14
προσευχή, Eph. 6:18
προσκαρτέρησις, Eph. 6:18
πρόσκλησις, I Tim. 5:21
πρόσκομμα, Rom. 9:32; 14:13, 20; I Cor. 8:9
προσκοπή, II Cor. 6:3
προστάτις, Rom. 16:2
προσφορά, Eph. 5:2
προσωπολημψία, Rom. 2:11; Eph. 6:9
πρόσωπον, I Cor. 13:12 (bis); 14:25; II Cor. 1:10; 3:18; 4:6;
    5:12; 8:23; 10:1, 7; 11:20; Gal. 2:6, 11; I Thess. 2:17;
    II Thess. 1:9
πρόφασις, Phil. 1:18; I Thess. 2:5
προφητεία, Rom. 12:6; I Cor. 12:10; 13:2, 8; 14:6; I Tim. 4:14
προφήτης, I Cor. 12:28, 29; 14:37; Eph. 4:11
πρωτότοκος, Rom. 8:29; Col. 1:15, 18
πτηνός, I Cor. 15:39
πτωχός, II Cor. 6:10
πῦρ, Rom. 12:20; I Cor. 3:13, 15; II Thess. 1:7

ῥάβδος, I Cor. 4:21
ῥῆμα, Rom. 10:17; II Cor. 12:4; Eph. 5:26; 6:18

ῥίζα, I Tim. 6:10
ῥιπή, I Cor. 15:52
ῥυτίς, Eph. 5:27

σαβαώθ, Rom. 9:29
σάββατον, Col. 2:16
σάλπινξ, I Thess. 4:16
σαρκικός, I Cor. 3:3 (bis)
σάρξ, Rom. 1:3; 2:28; 4:1; 8:3, 4, 5, 8, 9, 12, 13; 9:3, 5; I Cor. 1:26,
    29; 6:16; 10:18; 15:50; II Cor. 1:17; 5:16 (bis); 7:1; 10:2, 3
    (bis); Gal. 1:16; 2:20; 3:3; 4:23, 29; 5:16; 6:12; Eph. 2:11 (bis);
    5:31; 6:5, 12; Phil. 1:22; 3:3, 4, 5; Col. 2:1; 3:22; I Tim. 3:16;
    Philem. 16
Σατᾶν, II Cor. 12:7
σέβασμα, II Thess. 2:4
σελήνη, I Cor. 15:41
σεμνότης, I Tim. 2:2; 3:4
σημεῖον, Rom. 15:19; I Cor. 1:22; 14:22; II Cor. 12:12; II Thess.
    2:9; 3:17
σκάνδαλον, Rom. 9:32; 11:9; 14:13; I Cor. 1:23
σκέπασμα, I Tim. 6:8
σκεῦος, II Cor. 4:7; II Tim. 2:21
σκιά, Col. 2:17
σκοπός, Phil. 3:14
σκότος, Rom. 2:19; II Cor. 4:6; 6:14; Eph. 5:8; I Thess. 5:4, 6
σκύβαλον, Phil. 3:8
Σκύθης, Col. 3:11
σοφία, Rom. 11:33; I Cor. 1:17, 22, 24, 30; 2:1, 4, 5, 6 (ter), 13; 12:8;
    II Cor. 1:12; Eph. 1:8, 17; Col. 1:9, 28; 2:23; 3:16; 4:5
σοφός, Rom. 1:14; I Cor. 1:20, 26; 6:5; Eph. 5:15
σπέρμα, Rom. 1:3; 9:7 (bis), 8, 29; 11:1; II Cor. 9:10; 11:22; Gal.
    3:29; II Tim. 2:8
σπίλος, Eph. 5:27
σπλάγχνον, Phil. 1:8; 2:1; Col. 3:12
σπουδή, Rom. 12:8; II Cor. 7:11; 8:7
σταυρός, Phil. 2:8
στεῖρος, Gal. 4:27
στεναγμός, Rom. 8:26
στενοχωρία, Rom. 2:9; 8:35; II Cor. 6:4; 12:10
στέφανος, Phil. 4:1; I Thess. 2:19

στόμα, Rom. 10:10; II Cor. 13:1; II Tim. 4:17
στρατιώτης, II Tim. 2:3
στῦλος, Gal. 2:9; I Tim. 3:15
συζητητής, I Cor. 1:20
σύζυγος, Phil. 4:3
σύμβουλος, Rom. 11:34
συμμέτοχος, Eph. 3:6; 5:7
συμμιμητής, Phil. 3:17
συμπολίτης, Eph. 2:19
συμφώνησις, II Cor. 6:15
σύμφωνος, I Cor. 7:5
συγγνώμη, I Cor. 7:6
σύνδεσμος, Col. 3:14
συνείδησις, I Cor. 10:29; II Cor. 4:2; I Tim. 1:5, 19; 3:9; II Tim. 1:3
συνέκδημος, II Cor. 8:19
συνεργός, I Cor. 3:8; II Cor. 1:24; 8:23; Col. 4:11
σύνεσις, Col. 1:9; II Tim. 2:7
συνίων, Rom. 3:11
συνκατάθεσις, II Cor. 6:16
συνκληρονόμος, Rom. 8:17; Eph. 3:6
συνκοινωνός, Rom. 11:17
συνοχή, II Cor. 2:4
σύνσωμος, Eph. 3:6
σύντριμμα, Rom. 3:16
σφαγή, Rom. 8:36
σχῆμα, Phil. 2:8
σχίσμα, I Cor. 1:10, 18; 12:25
σῶμα, Rom. 12:4, 5; I Cor. 6:16; 10:17; 12:12, 13, 16, 20, 27; 15:35, 38 (bis); II Cor. 12:2, 3; Eph. 2:16; 4:4; Col. 2:23; 3:15
σωτήρ, Eph. 5:23; Phil. 3:20; I Tim. 1:1; 4:10; Titus 2:14
σωτηρία, Rom. 1:16; 10:1, 10; Phil. 1:19, 28; I Thess. 5:8, 9; II Thess. 2:13; II Cor. 6:2 (bis); 7:10; II Tim. 2:10; 3:15
σωφρονισμός, II Tim. 1:6
σωφροσύνη, I Tim. 2:9, 15

ταλαιπωρία, Rom. 3:16
τάξις, I Cor. 14:40
ταπεινοφροσύνη, Eph. 4:12; Col. 2:18, 23; 3:12
τάφος, Rom. 3:13
τάχος, Rom. 16:20

τεκνίον, Gal. 4:19

τέκνον, Rom. 8:16, 17; 9:7, 8; I Cor. 4:14, 17; II Cor. 6:13; Gal. 4:28,
 31; Eph. 2:3; 5:1, 9; Phil. 2:15, 22; I Thess. 2:12; I Tim. 1:1, 18;
 II Tim. 1:2; 2:1; Titus 1:4

τέλειος, I Cor. 14:20

τέλος, Rom. 10:4; II Cor. 1:13; I Thess. 2:16

τέρας, Rom. 15:19; II Cor. 12:12; II Thess. 2:9

τετράπους, Rom. 1:23

τήρησις, I Cor. 7:19

τιμή, Rom. 2:7, 10; 9:21; I Cor. 6:20; 7:23; 12:23, 24; Col. 2:23;
 I Thess. 4:4; I Tim. 1:17; 5:17; 6:1, 16; II Tim. 2:21 (bis)

τόπος, Rom. 15:23; Eph. 4:27

τρόμος, I Cor. 2:3; II Cor. 7:15; Eph. 6:5; Phil. 2:12; II Tim. 3:8

τροφός, I Thess. 2:7

τύπος, Rom. 5:14; I Cor. 10:6; Phil. 3:17; I Thess. 1:7; II Thess. 3:9;
 I Tim. 4:12; Titus 2:7

τυφλός, Rom. 2:19

ὕβρις, II Cor. 12:10

ὑβριστής, Rom. 1:30

υἱοθεσία, Rom. 8:15, 23; Eph. 1:5

υἱός, Rom. 1:4; 8:14; 9:26; II Cor. 6:18; Gal. 3:7, 26; 4:6, 7 (bis);
 I Thess. 5:5 (bis)

ὕμνος, Eph. 5:19; Col. 3:16

ὑπακοή, Rom. 1:5; 6:16 (bis); 15:18; 16:26

ὑπερβολή, Rom. 7:13; I Cor. 12:31; II Cor. 1:8; 4:17 (bis); Gal. 1:13

ὑπερήφανος, Rom. 1:30

ὑπεροχή, I Cor. 2:1; I Tim. 2:2

ὑπηρέτης, I Cor. 4:1

ὕπνος, Rom. 13:11

ὑπόκρισις, I Tim. 4:2

ὑπόμνησις, II Tim. 1:5

ὑπομονή, Rom. 2:7; 5:3; 8:25; II Cor. 1:6; 6:4; 12:12; Col. 1:11;
 I Tim. 6:11

ὑπόνοια, I Tim. 6:4

ὑποταγή, I Tim. 2:11; 3:4

ὑποτύπωσις, I Tim. 1:16; II Tim. 1:13

ὑστέρησις, Phil. 4:11

ὑψηλός, Rom. 11:20

ὕψος, Eph. 4:8

ὕψωμα, Rom. 8:39

Φαρισαῖος, Phil. 3:5
φαρμακία, Gal. 5:20
φθόνος, Rom. 1:29; Gal. 5:20; Phil. 1:15; I Tim. 6:4; Titus 3:3
φθορά, I Cor. 15:42; Gal. 6:8; Col. 2:22
φλόξ, II Thess. 1:7
φόβος, Rom. 3:18; 8:15; 13:3; I Cor. 2:3; II Cor. 7:1, 5, 11, 15;
    Eph. 5:21; 6:5; Phil. 2:12; I Tim. 5:20
φόνος, Rom. 1:29
φρεναπάτης, Titus 1:10
φρόνησις, Eph. 1:8
φυλακή, II Cor. 6:5; 11:23
φυλή, Rom. 11:1; Phil. 3:5
φύσις, Rom. 1:26; 2:14, 27; 11:21, 24 (ter); Gal. 2:15; 4:8; Eph. 2:3
φυσίωσις, II Cor. 12:20
φωνή, I Cor. 14:7; I Thess. 4:16
φῶς, Rom. 2:19; II Cor. 4:6; 6:14; 11:14; Eph. 5:8, 9, 13; I Thess.
    5:5; I Tim. 6:16
φωστήρ, Phil. 2:15
φωτισμός, II Cor. 4:6

χαίρων, Rom. 12:15
χαλκός, I Cor. 13:1
χαρά, Rom. 14:17; 15:13, 32; II Cor. 1:15; Gal. 5:22; Phil. 1:4; 2:29;
    4:1; I Thess. 1:6; II Tim. 1:5; Philem. 7
χάρις, Rom. 1:5, 7; 4:4, 16; 5:15; 6:14, 15, 17; 7:25; 11:5, 6; I Cor.
    1:3; 10:30; 15:10, 57; II Cor. 1:2, 12; 2:14; 8:16; 9:8, 15;
    Gal. 1:3, 6; Eph. 1:2; 2:5; 4:29; Phil. 1:2; Col. 1:2, 11; 3:16;
    4:6; I Thess. 1:1; 2:19; II Thess. 1:2; 2:16; I Tim. 1:2, 12;
    II Tim. 1:2, 3, 9; Titus 1:4; Philem. 3
χάρισμα, I Cor. 7:7; 12:4, 28, 30
χεῖλος, I Cor. 14:21
χειμών, II Tim. 4:20
χείρ, I Cor. 12:15; Gal. 3:19; I Tim. 5:22
χόρτος, I Cor. 3:12
χρεία, I Cor. 12:21, 24; I Thess. 1:8; 4:9, 12; 5:1
χρηστός, I Cor. 15:33
χρηστότης, Rom. 3:12; 11:22 (bis); II Cor. 6:6; Gal. 5:23; Eph. 2:7;
    Col. 3:12
Χριστός, Rom. 12:5; 16:5, 7, 9, 10; I Cor. 3:1; 4:10, 15; 6:15; Phil.
    1:21; 2:1; Col. 1:28; Philem. 8

Χριστός Ἰησοῦς, Rom. 16:3; I Cor. 4:15; Phil. 3:3; 4:19; I Thess. 2:14
χρόνος, Rom. 7:1; 16:25; II Tim. 1:9; Titus 1:2
χρυσίον, I Cor. 3:12; I Tim. 2:9

ψαλμός, Eph. 5:19; Col. 3:16
ψευδάδελφος, II Cor. 11:26
ψευδαπόστολος, II Cor. 11:13
ψευδολόγος, I Tim. 4:2
ψεῦδος, II Thess. 2:9
ψεύστης, Rom. 3:4; I Tim. 1:10; Titus 1:12
ψιθυρισμός, II Cor. 12:20
ψιθυριστής, Rom. 1:30
ψυχή, I Cor. 15:45; Eph. 6:7; Phil. 1:27; Col. 3:23
ψῦχος, II Cor. 11:27

ᾠδή, Eph. 5:19; Col. 3:16
ὥρα, Rom. 13:11; I Cor. 15:30; II Cor. 7:8; Gal. 2:5; I Thess. 2:17;
    Philem. 15

III. DETAILED STUDY OF SELECTED QUALITATIVE NOUNS

Νόμος

1. *Statistical and comparative statement of usage.*—This important word appears in Paul 117 times. It occurs frequently in some of the other New Testament literature, but is entirely absent from the Johannine Epistles and the Apocalypse, as well as from the Petrine Epistles and the Gospel of Mark. Outside the Pauline writings it is used generally with the article and with reference to the Mosaic law or to the Old Testament. For example, Matt. 12:5: "Or have ye not read in the law that on the Sabbath day the priests in the temple profane the Sabbath and are guiltless?" John 12:34: "We have heard out of the law that the Christ abideth forever." See also Luke 2:22; John 1:46; Acts 28:23; Heb. 9:22; Jas. 1:10. In Paul, however, νόμος frequently occurs qualitatively, with special emphasis upon the essential law quality of law, its "lawness," so to speak. Yet one must not fall into the error of thinking that it is always the legalistic quality of law that is prominent in the apostle's mind. In Rom. 13:10, πλήρωμα οὖν νόμου ἡ ἀγάπη, it is the ethical element of law which is to the fore. Νόμος used qualitatively presents this emphasis upon the essential character of law while at the same time designating it as the law referred to in the context. This is usually, but not invariably, the Mosaic law, and (*a*) the Mosaic law as a historic régime; (*b*) the Mosaic law legalistically interpreted; or (*c*) the Mosaic law ethically understood.[1]

Of the 117 instances in Paul, 46 are preceded by the article (usually restrictive), the context in the great majority of cases showing that the law referred to is that of the Old Testament. Among other instances may be cited: Rom. 2:14*b*, where the naturally lawless Gentiles are, credited with actions that are in accordance with the Jewish law; 2:20, where the Jew is represented as having or believing himself to have the form of knowledge and truth in the Law; 3:21, where it is affirmed

---

[1] To say that a noun is qualitative is not to deny to it specific reference to a particular thing. The function of a qualitative noun is not primarily to designate, but to lay stress upon the qualities of that to which the noun refers. In the case of νόμος the qualities are those that distinguish law, but the particular law in mind is usually the Mosaic law or the Old Testament in general, but this itself variously viewed as indicated above. Cf. Professor Ernest D. Burton, "Redemption from the Curse of the Law," *American Journal of Theology*, October, 1907, pp. 624–46.

that God's non-legal righteousness is attested by the Law and the Prophets.

In a few instances νόμος refers to some other code or statute defined in the context, or by metonymy to a force having an effect like that of a law. For example, Rom. 7:22–23: "For I delight in the law of God after the inward man; but I see a different law in my members, warring against the law of my mind, and bringing me into captivity under the law of sin which is in my members." See also Rom. 7:2, 3; 8:2a, et al.

2. *Usage in prepositional phrases.*—Of the 71 occurrences of νόμος without the article in the Pauline Epistles 35 are in prepositional phrases. From this fact it might be gathered that nouns in prepositional phrases tend to be qualitative. More extensive data are needed, however, to justify such an assumption. What is clear is that in Paul νόμος in prepositional phrases tends to be qualitative. In all the Pauline Epistles only 12 instances of νόμος with the article in prepositional phrases occur. In the rest of the New Testament the proportion is reversed, there being only 7 instances of anarthrous νόμος in prepositional phrases to 29 in which the article is used. The data as regards the prepositional usage of νόμος both with and without the article in the whole New Testament are as follows:

With the article:

ἀπὸ τοῦ νόμου (Matt. 5:18; Acts 28:23; Rom. 7:2, 3, 6; 8:2).

διὰ τοῦ νόμου (Rom. 7:5).

εἰς τὸν νόμον (Acts 25:8).

ἐκ τοῦ νόμου (John 12:34; Rom. 2:18; 4:16).

ἐν τῷ νόμῳ (Matt. 12:5; 22:36; Luke 2:24; 10:26; 24:44; John 1:46; 8:5, 17; 10:34; 15:25; Rom. 2:20; 7:23; I Cor. 9:9; 14:21).

κατὰ τοῦ νόμου (Acts 6:13; 21:28; Heb. 7:5).

κατὰ τὸν νόμον (Luke 2:22, 39; John 18:31; 19:7; Acts 23:3; 24:14; Heb. 9:19, 22).

μετὰ τὸν νόμον (Heb. 7:28).

παρὰ τὸν νόμον (Acts 18:13).

ὑπὸ τοῦ νόμου (Rom. 3:21; Jas. 2:9).

Without the article:

ἄχρι νόμου (Rom. 5:13).

διὰ νόμου (Rom. 2:12; 3:20, 27; 4:13; 7:7; Gal. 2:19, 21; Jas. 2:12).

εἰς νόμον (Rom. 9:31; Jas. 1:25).

ἐκ νόμου (Rom. 4:14; 10:5; Gal. 3:18, 21 [margin]; Phil. 3:9).

ἐν νόμῳ (Luke 2:23; Acts 13:39; Rom. 2:12, 23; Gal. 3:11, 21; 5:4; Phil. 3:6).

κατὰ νόμον (Phil. 3:5; Heb. 7:16; 8:4; 10:8).

περὶ νόμου (Acts 18:15).

ὑπὸ νόμου (Rom. 6:14, 15; I Cor. 9:20 (quater); Gal. 3:23; 4:4, 5, 21; 5:18).

χωρὶς νόμου (Rom. 3:21; 7:8, 9).

3. *Qualitative usage other than in prepositional phrases.*—Of the 71 anarthrous instances 61 are qualitative, the omission of the article having the effect, not of assigning the law referred to to a class of laws, as if it were one of many, but of emphasizing its quality as law. In many instances where the noun is limited by a qualifying genitive, itself anarthrous, it is the quality expressed by the whole compound expression, or especially that which is conveyed by the genitive which is emphasized.[1]

Numerous examples of the qualitative usage of νόμος might be presented and discussed. For example, Rom. 2:23a: ὃς ἐν νόμῳ καυχᾶσαι, διὰ τῆς παραβάσεως τοῦ νόμου τὸν θεὸν ἀτιμάζεις; Here in the prepositional phrase νόμος is qualitative. The Jew is represented as glorying in a religion whose distinguishing feature was its legalism. This legalistic character was as a matter of fact expressed in the Jewish code, but it is not here the code itself which the apostle has specially in mind but the legalistic nature of the Jewish religion. In the second half of the sentence, on the other hand, he refers to the code as such. When in the first clause the apostle says "thou who gloriest in law," it is obvious that if pressed to explain what law he had in mind he would have said "the Jewish law," but it is equally obvious that though making covert or unconscious reference to that law his primary emphasis is upon its essential characteristic as a legalistic system. The omission of the article in English in the first clause allows the intention of the Greek to make itself felt: "thou who gloriest in law, dost thou through thy transgression of the law dishonour God?"

Rom. 2:25 is another example: περιτομὴ μὲν γὰρ ὠφελεῖ ἐὰν νόμον πράσσῃς· ἐὰν δὲ παραβάτης νόμου ᾖς, ἡ περιτομή σου ἀκροβυστία γέγονεν. To bring out the qualitative force of νόμος here one might read "if thou be a law-keeper . . . . if thou be a law-transgressor," or "if thou be a keeper of law . . . . a transgressor of law." The insertion of the

---

[1] A qualitative noun may be modified by a noun which is itself qualitative, as, e.g., in Rom. 1:1, εὐαγγέλιον θεοῦ; 1:4, υἱοῦ θεοῦ; πνεῦμα ἁγιωσύνης; 2:29, περιτομὴ καρδίας; 7:25, νόμῳ θεοῦ . . . . νόμῳ ἁμαρτίας. In such collocations both words are qualitative, the stronger qualitative emphasis naturally lying upon the second term, the qualitative qualifier.

definite article in translation as in the Revised Version completely obliterates the qualitative usage and alters the sense of the passage.

Similarly in the oft-recurring phrase ἐξ ἔργων νόμου, while Paul no doubt has in mind the Old Testament Jewish law as the concrete thing by legalistic obedience tó which men were expecting to be justified, yet it is its quality as a legalistic system upon which he throws emphasis, and the proper translation would be "by works of law." So also in Rom. 7:25 we should read not "the law of God . . . . the law of sin," but "a law of God . . . . a law of sin."

In all these instances the qualitative usage of νόμος is clear and in some cases striking, particularly in passages where the qualitative and the definite usages stand side by side, as in Rom 2:14, 23 (already discussed); 3:21; Gal. 3:18–19; 4:21. Taking the last mentioned as a further illustration it is evident that the apostle's meaning is "tell me, ye that desire a legalistic type of religion, are ye not acquainted with the Jewish law?" or, more briefly, "ye that desire to be under law, do ye not hear the law?" Doubtless the "law" the legalistic Galatians wished to be "under" was actually the Mosaic law, but it is not that as such which Paul has in mind in the phrase "under law." That condition would be equally abhorrent to his mind whether it were the Mosaic or some other legalistic code. "Under law" meant actually in his own experience and doubtless in the Galatian tendency which he denounces specifically the Jewish law. Nevertheless it is not that or any other specific system which is designated by the phrase "under law" but the essential character of such systems, their law quality. Had the revisers rendered this passage with the insight that marked their translation of Rom. 6:14–15, where, amending the Authorized Version, they correctly read "for ye are not under law but under grace. What then? shall we sin because we are not under law but under grace?" the apostle's meaning would have been more adequately expressed.

Insistence upon the recognition of the qualitative force of νόμος in Paul is more than a mere grammatical punctilio; it is a necessary element in correct interpretation. Its recognition enlarges the apostle's religious philosophy from an anti-codal polemic to a wide-sweeping assertion of spiritual freedom. He insisted on absolute spiritual liberty, and his breach with legal morality was complete. To limit his reference to the Mosaic code alone is in many instances to reduce the force of his statement and to narrow his thought. Other excellent specimens of the qualitative use of νόμος are found in the following passages: Luke 2:23; Rom. 2:23; Gal. 2:21; 3:2; 5:4; Phil. 3:6; Heb. 10:8.

4. *The Revised Version renderings of νόμος.*—In the translation of this word the revisers have generally ignored the distinction between the definite ὁ νόμος and the qualitative νόμος in so far as the latter is concerned.[1] When the context makes it reasonably clear that it is the Mosaic law that Paul has especially in mind they have taken this as warrant for translating νόμος "the law," obscuring the fact that his emphasis is upon its law quality.

The insertion in some instances of alternative readings bears witness to the revisers' uncertainty and increases the difficulty of interpretation on the basis of the English text. In the following conspectus the Revised Version renderings of anarthrous νόμος in the Pauline literature are divided into two groups, viz., those passages in which a text reading and a marginal reading are given, and those passages in which a text reading only is given. These are then subdivided into their various possibilities. Carried out to its fullest extent the conspectus would present a series of 27, based upon the possible choices between the text and marginal readings of "law," "a law," and "the law." To present this series in full is unnecessary, inasmuch as only a few of these possibilities are actually adopted by the revisers. The arrangement of the facts presented is, however, such that in every passage in the Pauline Epistles where νόμος appears without the article the single correct rendering is indicated, together with the Revised Version's divergences therefrom where such occur. By this means it is hoped the conspectus may be of value to the New Testament interpreter in the field which it covers.

1. Anarthrous νόμος is rendered by "the law" in the text and "law" in the margin: (a) When the marginal reading should have stood in the text (Rom. 3:20 [*bis*], 28, 31 [*bis*]; 4:13; 5:20; 7:1a, 7b, 8, 9). (b) When the rendering should have been "a law": no instance. (c) Correctly: no instance.

2. Anarthrous νόμος is rendered by a single text reading as follows: (a) By "law": (i) When the rendering should have been "a law"; in no instance. (ii) When the rendering should have been "the law"; in no instance. (iii) Correctly (Rom. 3:27a; 6:14, 15; 7:2a; I Tim. 1:9). (b) By "a law": (i) When the rendering should have been "the law"; in no instance. (ii) When the rendering should have been "law" (Rom. 9:31a). (iii) Correctly[2] (Rom. 3:27b; 4:15; 5:13;

[1] For cases of inaccurate translation see Rom. 2:17, 25; 3:20, 21a, 31; 4:13, 14; 5:13, 20; 7:1, 7b, 8; 10:4, 5; 13:8; I Cor. 9:20; Gal. 2:16 (*bis*), 19, 21; 3:2, 10, 11, 18, 21c, 23; 4:4, 5, 21a; 5:4, 18; 6:13; Phil. 3:5, 6, 9.

[2] In Rom. 4:15; 5:13; Gal. 5:23, "no law" is regarded as equivalent to "not a" or "not any law."

7:23*a;* Gal. 5:23). (*c*) By "the law": (i) When the rendering should have been "a law"; in no instance. (ii) When the rendering should have been "law" (Rom. 2:12 [*bis*], 13 [*bis*], 14 [*ter*], 17, 23, 25 [*bis*]; 3:21*a;* 4:14; 5:13; 7:25 [*bis*]; 9:31*b*;[1] 10:4, 5; 13:8, 10; I Cor. 9:20 [*quater*]; Gal. 2:16 [*ter*], 19 [*bis*], 21; 3:2, 5, 10, 11, 18, 21 [*bis*], 23; 4:4, 5, 21; 5:4, 18; 6:13; Phil. 3:5, 6). (iii) Correctly; in no instance.

While the larger number of the foregoing possibilities are merely theoretical and actual instances of such translations do not occur, it is important to exhibit them; and that their failure to appear is not due to any intrinsic improbability or to the watchfulness of the revisers is indicated by the large number of instances, viz., 48, in which νόμος is translated "the law" when a correct rendering would have required "law."

In the 11 instances where the revisers were in doubt or disagreement among themselves as to whether the rendering should be "the law" or "law" they have in every instance placed the wrong rendering "the law" in the text and the correct reading "law" in the margin.[2] In one instance they have read "a law" where the rendering should have been "law." In one instance the anarthrous and qualitative νόμος has been incorrectly rendered "that law"; in 5 instances they have read "a law" correctly, and in 5 they have read "law" correctly. Thus out of 71 instances of anarthrous νόμος, 61 are palpable mistranslations, though in 11 of these the correct rendering is given in the margin. That the obviously qualitative Pauline usage of this word could so completely fail of recognition in the revision of the New Testament is an evidence of the need that New Testament interpreters, either on the basis of the Greek or the English text, give attention to the qualitative usage of nouns; it is moreover a sufficient apology for such an investigation as the one here presented.[3]

Ἁμαρτία

1. *Statistical and comparative statement of usage.*—This word bulks largely in the Pauline writings, though not, perhaps, excessively, con-

[1] In Rom. 9:31*b* εἰς νόμον οὐκ ἔφθασεν is translated "did not arrive at *that* law."

[2] It is to be noted that the 11 instances where an alternative reading is suggested are in no way different from the 48 instances where the reading "the law" was chosen without such marginal variation. The consistent rendering of anarthrous νόμος as a definitive noun evidently proceeds upon the assumption that νόμος refers definitely and almost exclusively to the law of Moses. This assumption overlooks its qualitative character and fails to account for the absence of the article.

[3] In all instances where νόμος with the article occurs in the Pauline Epistles it is correctly rendered "the law."

sidering their nature and extent. It occurs 61 times in the Pauline Epistles. About one-third of its occurrences in the New Testament are in Paul, and two-thirds of those in Paul are in Romans.

'Αμαρτία occurs much more frequently with the article than without it. With the article it is used commonly in the generic sense; so, for example, in Rom. 5:12: "Therefore, as by one man sin [ἡ ἁμαρτία] entered into the world," etc.; also Rom. 6:13: "Neither present your members unto sin [τῇ ἁμαρτίᾳ] as instruments of unrighteousness," etc. A few instances, however, of the restrictive usage occur; so, e.g., I Cor. 15:3: "Christ died for our sins" (ὑπὲρ τῶν ἁμαρτιῶν ἡμῶν); also vs. 17: "Ye are yet in your sins" (ἐν ταῖς ἁμαρτίαις ὑμῶν); see also Gal. 1:4.

'Αμαρτία occurs without the article in the Pauline Epistles 20 times, viz., Rom. 3:9, 20; 4:8; 5:13 (bis); 6:14, 16; 7:7, 8, 13; 8:3 (bis), 10; 14:23; II Cor. 5:21; 11:7; Gal. 2:17; 3:22; I Tim. 5:22; II Tim. 3:6. In 4 of the foregoing instances of anarthrous ἁμαρτία the noun is used indefinitely; so, e.g., II Cor. 11:7: "Or did I commit a sin [ἁμαρτίαν] in abasing myself that ye may be exalted?" See also II Cor. 5:21; I Tim. 5:22; II Tim. 3:6. The remaining 16 instances of anarthrous ἁμαρτία are examples of qualitative usage and will be more fully discussed under that head.

2. *Usage in prepositional phrases.*—Four instances of ἁμαρτία without the article in prepositional phrases occur in the Pauline Epistles. In each instance the term is qualitative. The passages are as follows: διὰ ἁμαρτίαν (Rom. 8:10); περὶ ἁμαρτίας (Rom. 8:3b); ὑπὸ ἁμαρτίαν (Rom. 3:9; Gal. 3:22). In all the above the indefinite sense is manifestly excluded. Had the author desired he might conceivably have inserted the article and have used the word in the generic sense. What he in fact did was to use the noun in every case in such a way as to throw emphasis upon the character and qualities of sin. In every case it is not sin conceived of generically as including every form of evil action, nor is it any particular evil act, but sin thought of with reference to its evil characteristics that is prominent in the apostle's mind. This qualitative shade is with difficulty reproduced in the English, vocal stress upon the word "sin" being perhaps as near an approximation to the force of the original as could be given by a more laborious circumlocution or paraphrase.

Eight instances of ἁμαρτία with the article in prepositional phrases are found in the Pauline Epistles, as follows: ἀπὸ τῆς ἁμαρτίας (Rom. 6:7, 18, 22); διὰ τῆς ἁμαρτίας (Rom. 5:12); ἐν ταῖς ἁμαρτίαις (I Cor. 15:17);

ὑπὲρ τῶν ἁμαρτιῶν (I Cor. 15:3; Gal. 1:4); ὑπὸ τὴν ἁμαρτίαν (Rom. 7:14). In 5 of the foregoing instances, viz., Rom. 5:12; 6:7, 18, 22; 7:14, ἁμαρτία is used with the article in the generic sense, in the other 3 (I Cor. 15:3, 17; Gal. 1:4) it is used restrictively. In so far as the data furnished by the Pauline Epistles justify an inference the fact would seem to be that the apostle makes a clear discrimination in prepositional phrases, as elsewhere, between ἁμαρτία regarded as a generic term and ἁμαρτία thought of as respects the qualities belonging to that which is so named, indicating this discrimination by the omission and insertion of the article. In other words, the prepositional phrase offers no exception to the rule that nouns with the article are either restrictive or generic, while anarthrous nouns are either indefinite or qualitative. It may well be that prepositional phrases by their very nature are more frequently qualitative than not, though a separate and exhaustive investigation would be required to establish that conclusion; but the fact here observed is that the lines of demarcation between both the nouns with the article and the anarthrous noun and also between the two uses of the anarthrous noun obtain in prepositional phrases as well as in independent constructions.

3. *Qualitative usage other than in prepositional phrases.*—There are 12 instances of the qualitative usage of ἁμαρτία aside from those occurring in prepositional phrases which remain to be considered. They are Rom. 3:20; 4:8; 5:13 (*bis*); 6:14, 16; 7:7, 8, 13; 8:3a; 14:23; Gal. 2:17. Of these several outstanding examples are selected for more detailed discussion. The qualitative character that is so prominent in these is, however, discernible in every one of the twelve.

Rom. 7:7: ὁ νόμος ἁμαρτία; Here Paul repudiates a conceived consequence of his reasoning by an argumentative question which states at once the objector's assumption and his own protest thereagainst. The apostle's query is not whether the Jewish law is of such a nature that from some conceivable point of view it may be looked upon as classifiable under the category of sins; it is whether the law may be affirmed those qualities which are characteristic of sin. This distinction is subtle, for if a thing is a sin it is evident that it will possess characteristics which sin possesses. Conversely, the possession of such characteristics would appear to justify its relegation to the category of sins. Though the qualitative and indefinite usages here approximate, they remain distinct, the emphasis lying upon the possession of attributes, ἁμαρτία describing by the ascription of qualities and not designating by assignment to a class.

Rom. 7:13: ἀλλὰ ἡ ἁμαρτία, ἵνα φανῇ ἁμαρτία, κτλ. In this striking passage the generic and qualitative usages appear in conjunction. The qualitative emphasis of the anarthrous ἁμαρτία is comparable to ἁμαρτωλός in capitals, were such a method of indicating emphasis allowable in Greek. The thought is repeated in the next clause by another construction, the two in this immediate collocation affording an impressive example of the adjectival equivalence of qualitative usage. Rearranging the second clause in the order of the first, for the purpose of comparison, we have ἡ ἁμαρτία, ἵνα φανῇ ἁμαρτία, κτλ. ἡ ἁμαρτία ἵνα γένηται καθ' ὑπερβολὴν ἁμαρτωλός, κτλ. Paul's thought is that under the circumstances which he narrates the essential qualities and characteristics of sin emerge. Sin now appears as sin, whatever it may have seemed before; that is to say, in the anarthrous ἁμαρτία the emphasis in the apostle's thought is not upon sin thought of abstractly or in general, nor is it upon any particular sin, but upon the inherently evil characteristics of sin, the qualities that make sin sin.

Rom. 14:23 further illustrates the qualitative usage of ἁμαρτία: πᾶν δὲ ὃ οὐκ ἐκ πίστεως ἁμαρτία ἐστίν. The statement of the apostle is not that whatsoever is not "of faith" is a sin, that is, may be reckoned as one in the catalogue of sins; it is the affirmation that of whatsoever is not "of faith" sin qualities are to be predicated.

English idiom commonly, though not always, makes the indefinite and the qualitative uses of the word "sin" identical in form, differentiating them by a difference of vocal stress. For example, in enumerating the Montanist catalogue of mortal sins one might mention idolatry, fraud, denial of the faith, blasphemy, adultery, and fornication. Upon being reminded that there were seven, one might say, "Oh, yes, homicide is a sin, too." In such sentences as "avarice is a sin," "theft is a sin," all that is affirmed of these vices is that they are to be classed under the common title "sin." But in sentences like the following such is not the case. For example, "the neglect of civic duties is a sin"; "the military unpreparedness of the United States is a sin"; "the exploitation of the ignorant is a sin." In these sentences the intention of the user is not to affirm that the various acts and conditions in question are members of the class sin; it is to say that of these acts and conditions qualities may be predicated which may also be predicated of sin. Here, again, the distinction between the indefinite and the qualitative usages appears to vanish in fact but it is preserved in thought, the term "sin" being descriptive rather than designative and drawing attention to attributes rather than classifying by relegation to a category.

4. *The Revised Version renderings of* ἁμαρτία.—In all the instances where ἁμαρτία with the article is used generically the Revised Version, in accordance with English idiom, translates without the article. In the few examples of the restrictive which occur, which are in every case in the plural and modified by a following possessive pronoun, English idiom is such that the article naturally does not appear in the translation. In the 4 cases where ἁμαρτία is used indefinitely the Revised Version rendering is appropriate. In II Cor. 5:21 indefinite and qualitative usages occur side by side: τὸν μὴ γνόντα ἁμαρτίαν ὑπὲρ ἡμῶν ἁμαρτίαν ἐποίησεν. The first ἁμαρτία is probably indefinite, the intention being to affirm the sinlessness of Christ and this by the statement that he did not know experientially any single sin. The second ἁμαρτία is clearly qualitative. Obviously no single sin is meant. The argument is that the Christ who was guiltless of any single sin was regarded and treated by God as if possessing the qualities that sin possesses. This is fairly rendered by "Him who knew no sin he made to be sin on our behalf," where the words, "no sin" may be regarded as equivalent to "not a sin." In the case of the first ἁμαρτία, however, it is difficult to determine whether the intention is indefinite or qualitative. Cf. Eph. 2:12; I Thess. 4:13.

In all cases where ἁμαρτία without the article is used qualitatively the Revised Version renderings are such as not to obscure in the English the design of the anarthrous usage in the Greek. In Rom. 8:3a the phrase σὰρξ ἁμαρτίας is rendered "sinful flesh," thus emphasizing the qualitative force of the term. In Gal. 2:17 ἆρα Χριστὸς ἁμαρτίας διάκονος; is properly translated "Is Christ a minister of sin?" and by a vocal inflection the qualitative force of ἁμαρτία may be made evident in the English. Here, too, is an example of a qualitative noun modified by another qualitative noun, the whole phrase being qualitative, but the chief qualitative contribution being made by the qualitative qualifier.

In general it may be said that the Revised Version renderings of both ἡ ἁμαρτία and ἁμαρτία are in all cases faithful to the Greek and are such as to enable the interpreter of the English text to express by vocal emphasis the qualitative character of the noun, although that qualitative character must first be discovered by a study of the Greek.

Πίστις

1. *Statistical and comparative statement of usage.*—As one of the most frequent and important New Testament as well as Pauline terms, this word is deserving of special attention. About three-fifths of all the

instances occurring in the New Testament are in the Pauline Epistles, Romans and Galatians, in keeping with their doctrinal and argumentative character, furnishing the largest numbers. Πίστις occurs with comparative infrequency in the restrictive sense (cf. I Tim. 1:19; 6:10, 21; II Tim. 3:8; Titus 1:13; I Cor. 16:13; II Cor. 13:5), commonly in the generic, occasionally in the qualitative, and probably never in the indefinite sense. It occurs most frequently in Paul in prepositional phrases, an exhibition of whose usage is appended. Its use in the qualitative sense otherwise than in prepositional phrases is extremely rare.

2. *Usage in prepositional phrases.*—The following is a list of the passages in the New Testament in which πίστις is used after a preposition: With the article:

ἀπὸ τῆς πίστεως (Acts 13:8; I Tim. 8:10).

διὰ τῆς πίστεως (Rom. 1:12; 3:30, 31; Gal. 3:14, 26; Eph. 3:12, 17; Col. 2:12; I Thess. 3:7; Heb. 11:39).

εἰς τὴν πίστιν (Gal. 3:23).

ἐν τῇ πίστει (I Cor. 16:13; II Cor. 13:5; Titus 1:13; II Pet. 1:15).

ἐπὶ τῇ πίστει (Phil. 3:9).

κατὰ τὴν πίστιν (Matt. 9:29).

περὶ τῆς πίστεως (Acts 24:34; I Tim. 1:19).

περὶ τὴν πίστιν (I Tim. 6:21; II Tim. 3:8).

ὑπὲρ τῆς πίστεως (I Thess. 3:2; II Thess. 1:4).

Without the article:

διὰ πίστεως (Rom. 3:22, 25; II Cor. 5:7; Gal. 2:16; Eph. 2:8; Phil. 3:9; II Tim. 3:15; Heb. 1:12; 11:33; I Pet. 1:5).

εἰς πίστιν (Rom. 1:17).

ἐκ πίστεως (Rom. 1:17 [*bis*]; 3:26, 30; 4:16 [*bis*]; 5:1; 9:30, 32; 10:6; 14:23 [*bis*]; Gal. 2:16; 3:7, 8, 9, 11, 12, 22, 24; 5:5; I Tim. 1:5; Heb. 10:38; Jas. 2:24).

ἐν πίστει (Gal. 2:20; II Thess. 2:13; I Tim. 1:2, 4; 2:7, 15; 3:13; 4:12; II Tim. 1:13; Titus 3:15; Jas. 1:6).

κατὰ πίστιν (Titus 1:1; Heb. 11:7, 13).

μετὰ πίστεως (Eph. 6:23; I Tim. 1:14).

χωρὶς πίστεως (Heb. 11:6).

Upon the basis of these data the following observations may be made:

1. The expression ἐκ πίστεως is almost exclusively a Pauline phrase. In Heb. 10:38 it is taken from the Old Testament (Hab. 2:4), and in Jas. 2:24 one can almost see the defiant quotation marks on it. One might punctuate it ἐξ ἔργων δικαιοῦται ἄνθρωπος καὶ οὐκ "ἐκ πίστεως"

μόνον. Cf. Rom. 3:28. In I Tim. 1:5 ἐκ . . . . πίστεως is a non-Pauline usage and has no technical sense.

2. Though Paul says ἐκ πίστεως so frequently he never says ἐκ τῆς πίστεως.

3. On the other hand διὰ πίστεως and διὰ τῆς πίστεως occur with about equal frequency. In the 10 cases where διὰ τῆς πίστεως occurs 6 are clearly restrictive, 2 are possibly so, that is, the article may be equivalent to a possessive pronoun. This, while not decisive, may offer presumptive evidence that in the 2 cases in Rom 3:30 the article is restrictive and in that case directs the thought to the previous qualitative instances, the expression then meaning "the faith" (i.e., the faith we are discussing). If this is so the usage of πίστις in prepositional phrases shows no deviation from the regular usage of nouns in other constructions.

3. *Qualitative usage other than in prepositional phrases.*—In the Pauline Epistles, as has been remarked, anarthrous πίστεως in other than prepositional constructions is of relatively infrequent occurrence. It is, however, so used in the following 20 instances: Rom. 1:5; 3:27, 28; 4:13; 12:3; 14:22; 16:26; I Cor. 12:9; 13:13; Gal. 3:2, 5; 5:6, 22; Eph. 4:5; I Thess. 5:8; II Thess. 1:11; 2:13; I Tim. 6:11; II Tim. 2:22; Titus 2:10. In none of the above can the usage be shown to be indefinite. In every case the usage is qualitative.

As outstanding examples of the qualitative usage of πίστις may be quoted (Rom. 3:27): διὰ ποίου νόμου; τῶν ἔργων; οὐχί, ἀλλὰ διὰ νόμου πίστεως. Here is an instance of the qualitative noun as the modifier of another qualitative noun. It is the quality of πίστις in the νόμος πίστεως which in the apostle's mind makes boasting impossible. The theory of justification through meritorious action permits or encourages self-gratulation; the law of faith (i.e., the law which calls for faith), upon which he insists, excludes it. And it is because of its faith quality that the principle for which he contends produces this result. Πίστις is therefore strongly qualitative.

A similar qualitative emphasis is seen in the use of πίστις in Rom. 4:13: Οὐ γὰρ διὰ νόμου ἡ ἐπαγγελία τῷ Ἀβραὰμ . . . . ἀλλὰ διὰ δικαιοσύνης πίστεως. Here νόμου is set in contrast with δικαιοσύνης, not with the δικαιοσύνης which is the issue of the observance of legal requirements but a δικαιοσύνης which is the product of faith. This contrast of nomic and pistic righteousness is accomplished by the use of πίστις qualitatively. The righteousness alluded to is a faith righteousness, and πίστις is so used as to lay stress upon its qualities as faith in distinction from the qualities possessed by law.

4. *The Revised Version renderings of πίστις.*—In their translation of πίστις used qualitatively the revisers have in general given opportunity only for acquiescent criticism. In Rom. 4:16b they have inserted the definite article where the qualitative force both of πίστις and the rare instance of a proper noun used qualitatively might, perhaps, be more clearly expressed by the rendering "by Abrahamic faith." The renderings of πίστις in prepositional phrases in the Revised Version are, with one possible exception (Titus 1:1), such as to bring out the qualitative force. The insertion of the article by the revisers gives the term in this passage a definiteness which the Greek does not justify.

Δικαιοσύνη

1. *Statistical and comparative statement of usage.*—Out of a total of 58 occurrences in the Pauline Epistles 22 have the article and 36 are anarthrous. Of the 36 anarthrous instances all but one (Phil. 3:9) are qualitative, the usage in no case being clearly indefinite. In Phil. 3:9, though no article occurs, the sense is definite, the noun preceded by a possessive personal pronoun being equivalent to τὴν δικαιοσύνην μου. Of the 35 qualitative instances 15 are in prepositional phrases and 20 are in independent constructions. No instance of δικαιοσύνη with the article in a prepositional phrase occurs in the New Testament.

2. *Usage in prepositional phrases.*—The prepositional usage of the whole New Testament is as follows: διὰ δικαιοσύνης (Rom. 4:13; 5:21; 8:10; I Pet. 3:14); εἰς δικαιοσύνην (Rom. 4:3, 5, 9, 22; 6:16; 10:4, 10; Gal. 3:6; Jas. 2:23); ἐν δικαιοσύνῃ (Luke 1:75; Acts 17:31; Eph. 4:24; 5:9; II Tim. 3:16; II Pet. 1:1; Rev. 19:11); κατὰ δικαιοσύνην (Phil. 3:6); περὶ δικαιοσύνης (John 16:8, 10; Acts 24:25). In all these cases the qualitative force either of the term or of the phrase of which the term is a part is obvious.

3. *Qualitative usage other than in prepositional phrases.*—Of the 20 instances of qualitative usage in constructions other than prepositional phrases a few may be cited as typical:

Rom. 3:5: εἰ δὲ ἡ ἀδικία ἡμῶν θεοῦ δικαιοσύνην συνίστησιν, τί ἐροῦμεν; "But if our unrighteousness commendeth the righteousness of God, what shall we say?" Here the unrighteousness of man is set in contrast with the divine righteousness. Were the sense not qualitative and the intention merely contrast we should expect to find δικαιοσύνη used restrictively. The absence of the article with both δικαιοσύνη and θεοῦ indicates that both are used qualitatively. In the case of neither is there any indefiniteness, as if there were a δικαιοσύνη τοῦ θεοῦ and a δικαιοσύνη τῶν ἀνθρώπων or

47

τῶν ἀγγέλων. The sense of the combined words is divine "righteousness." Similar examples occur in Rom. 1:17; 3:21, 22; 4:6.

Rom. 6:13: ἀλλὰ παραστήσατε . . . . τὰ μέλη ὑμῶν ὅπλα δικαιοσύνης τῷ θεῷ. "But present . . . . your members as instruments of righteousness unto God." Here δικαιοσύνη is used as an anarthrous genitive modifier. It is clearly qualitative, the intention being to call the reader's attention to the distinctively righteous character of the "weapons" yielded to God or to the righteous result produced by God's use of them. Conceivably δικαιοσύνη might have had the article and have been either generic or restrictive. Being anarthrous its reference is clearly qualitative.

Rom. 9:30: Τί οὖν ἐροῦμεν; ὅτι ἔθνη τὰ μὴ διώκοντα δικαιοσύνην κατέλαβεν δικαιοσύνην, δικαιοσύνην δὲ τὴν ἐκ πίστεως. "What shall we say then? That the Gentiles, who followed not after righteousness, attained to righteousness, even the righteousness which is of faith."[1] In the first of these instances the usage is clearly qualitative, the second might be thought to be indefinite, the third restrictive. It is possible, however, that all three are qualitative. The passages illustrate the difficulty that sometimes attends the identification of qualitative usage.

II Cor. 5:21: τὸν μὴ γνόντα ἁμαρτίαν ὑπὲρ ἡμῶν ἁμαρτίαν ἐποίησεν, ἵνα ἡμεῖς γενώμεθα δικαιοσύνη θεοῦ ἐν αὐτῷ. "Him who knew no sin he made to be sin on our behalf: that we might become the righteousness of God in him." God's imputation of sin to Christ allows the imputation of divine righteousness to us. Both sin (5:21b) and righteousness are used qualitatively. Cf. note on ἁμαρτία.

II Cor. 11:15: οὐ μέγα οὖν εἰ καὶ οἱ διάκονοι αὐτοῦ μετασχηματίζονται ὡς διάκονοι δικαιοσύνης. "It is no great thing, therefore, if his ministers also fashion themselves as ministers of righteousness." The qualitative sense of δικαιοσύνη is very clear; the διάκονοι Σατανᾶ are naturally thought of as διάκονοι ἀδικίας but are apparently transformed into beings whose labors are directed toward the production of righteousness.

4. *The Revised Version renderings of* δικαιοσύνη.—In the translation of this word when used qualitatively in prepositional phrases the Revised Version wrongly inserts the article in Rom 4:13; II Pet. 1:1. In independent constructions (Rom. 1:17) it inserts the indefinite article as if God's righteousness were conceived of by the apostle as of several sorts. Similarly in Rom. 3:5 the insertion of the definite article emphasizes the class to which the righteousness belongs, which in the Greek is

---

[1] Note the qualitative use of the gentilic noun ἔθνη and its mistranslation in the English. How much more forceful had the article been omitted in the translation!

expressed by the precedence of θεοῦ, but weakens the implication of quality which the omission of the article with δικαιοσύνη indicates. In Rom. 3:21 it exhibits a striking negligence, ignoring again the qualitative character of the term and making it indefinite; in 4:3, 5, 6, 9, however, the qualitative character is adequately rendered; in II Cor. 5:21 it inserts the definite article, thus modifying the qualitative force appreciably; in Rom. 4:22, 5:21, and 8:10, on the other hand, the qualitative effect is preserved. In Rom. 9:30 a notable example of the collocation of the definite and qualitative usages occurs and the Revised Version renders both appropriately. Other instances of the correct rendering of δικαιοσύνη used qualitatively could be adduced. In its translation the revisers have not been uniform in their renderings, affording opportunity for criticism in some cases but oftener adhering to the spirit of the Greek. In many of these, it must be admitted, no special discernment was required, and a literal translation of the Greek was both the most obvious rendering and at the same time sufficient expression of the qualitative effect in English.

Ἐλπίς

1. *Statistical and comparative statement of usage.*—Ἐλπίς occurs 36 times in Paul, 15 times with the article and 21 times without it.

When used with the article it is in the following 6 cases generic: Rom. 5:5; 8:24a; 12:12; 15:4, 13 (*bis*). In the following 9 cases it is restrictive: II Cor. 1:6; Eph. 1:18; Phil. 1:20; Col. 1:5, 23, 27; I Thess. 1:3; I Tim. 1:1; Titus 2:13. As an example of the generic usage may be cited Rom. 5:5: "And hope [ἡ ἐλπίς] maketh not ashamed." As an example of the restrictive usage may be cited Col. 1:5: "because of the hope which is laid up for you in the heavens."

When used without the article ἐλπίς is in the following 3 cases probably indefinite: Rom. 8:24b; II Cor. 3:12 (see, however, Matt. 8:10, τοσαύτην πίστιν); Eph. 4:4. In the following 18 cases it is qualitative: Rom. 4:18 (*bis*); 5:2, 4; 8:20, 24c; I Cor. 9:10 (*bis*); 13:13; II Cor. 10:15; Gal. 5:5; Eph. 2:12 (cf. II Cor. 5:21, where ἁμαρτία was reckoned indefinite); I Thess. 2:19; 4:13; 5:8; II Thess. 2:16; Titus 1:2; 3:7. As an example of the indefinite usage may be cited Eph. 4:4: "There is one body and one spirit, even as ye also were called in one hope of your calling." Examples of the qualitative usage will be discussed under that head.

2. *Usage in prepositional phrases.*—Ἐλπίς occurs 13 times in prepositional phrases in the Pauline writings, in 4 cases with the article and in 9 cases without it.

When used with the article it is in one case generic, viz., Rom. 15:13: "That ye may abound in hope" (ἐν τῇ ἐλπίδι). In the following three cases it is restrictive: Phil. 1:20; Col. 1:4, 23. As an example of the restrictive usage may be cited Col. 1:23: "and not moved away from the hope [ἀπὸ τῆς ἐλπίδος] of the gospel which ye heard." In one instance anarthrous ἐλπίς in a prepositional phrase is used indefinitely, viz., Eph. 4:4: "There is one body and one spirit, even as ye were called in one hope [ἐν μιᾷ ἐλπίδι] of your calling."

In the following 8 instances ἐλπίς without the article is used qualitatively: Rom. 4:18 (bis); 5:2; 8:20; I Cor. 9:10 (bis); Titus 1:2; 3:7.

The following conspectus exhibits the complete prepositional usage of ἐλπίς in the Pauline Epistles:

With the article:

ἀπὸ τῆς ἐλπίδος (Col. 1:23).

διὰ τὴν ἐλπίδα (Col. 1:5).

ἐν τῇ ἐλπίδι (Rom. 15:13).

κατὰ . . . . τὴν ἐλπίδα (Phil. 1:20).

Without the article:

ἐν μιᾷ ἐλπίδι (Eph. 4:4).

ἐπ' ἐλπίδι (Rom. 4:18; 5:2; 8:20; I Cor. 9:10 [bis]; Titus 1:2).

κατ' ἐλπίδα (Titus 3:7).

παρ' ἐλπίδα (Rom. 4:18).

3. *Qualitative usage other than in prepositional phrases.*—Ἐλπίς, when anarthrous, is qualitative in 18 out of 21 instances. This is not to deny, as has been previously remarked, that the term, while thus qualitative, may have a definite reference. In I Thess. 4:13, for example, καθὼς καὶ οἱ λοιποὶ οἱ μὴ ἔχοντες ἐλπίδα doubtless refers especially to the Christian hope of a future life, while the usage is such as to throw stress upon the characteristics of that hope rather than upon its identity. In Rom. 8:24 a concurrence of the generic, the indefinite, and the qualitative uses of ἐλπίς is found: τῇ γὰρ ἐλπίδι ἐσώθημεν· ἐλπὶς δὲ βλεπομένη οὐκ ἔστιν ἐλπίς. Here the first ἐλπίς is generic, the second indefinite, and the third qualitative. The writer's thought is that a hope once realized ceases to have the character of hope but takes on that of experience. While this is perhaps the most striking instance of the qualitative usage of ἐλπίς, the same qualitative intent is discernible in all the instances cited.

4. *The Revised Version renderings of ἐλπίς.*—The translation of ἐλπίς used qualitatively is almost without exception such as to offer no occasion for demurring criticism. In Gal. 5:5 and I Thess. 5:8 the insertion of the article tends to obscure the qualitative character of the

Greek expression. At the same time it is difficult, if not impossible, to preserve in English both the definite and the qualitative tinges which are present in the phrases ἐλπὶς δικαιοσύνης and ἐλπὶς σωτηρίας. If in the translation the one is lost the other at least is preserved. The simple omission of the article in these passages would have made passable English and would have allowed the qualitative emphasis to be felt in the translation. Notable examples of felicitous rendering of the qualitative usage may be observed in Rom. 8:24 and II Thess. 2:16.

Εὐαγγέλιον

1. *Statistical and comparative statement of usage.*—It is sometimes remarked that this term is a favorite with Paul. Of its 75 occurrences in the New Testament 59 are in the Pauline Epistles. It is in all but 3 cases preceded by the article, and when so preceded is always restrictive. Of the 3 examples of anarthrous usage (Rom. 1:1; II Cor. 11:4; Gal. 1:6) all are qualitative.

2. *Usage in prepositional phrases.*—A complete exhibit of the usage of εὐαγγέλιον in the whole New Testament is as follows:
With the article:

διὰ τὸ εὐαγγέλιον (I Cor. 9:23).

διὰ τοῦ εὐαγγελίου (I Cor. 4:15; Eph. 3:16; II Thess. 2:14; II Tim. 1:10).

εἰς τὸ εὐαγγέλιον (II Cor. 2:12; 9:13; Phil. 1:5; 2:22).

ἐκ τοῦ εὐαγγελίου (I Cor. 9:14).

ἐν τῷ εὐαγγελίῳ (Mark 1:15; Rom. 1:9; I Cor. 9:18; II Cor. 8:18; 10:14; Phil. 4:3; I Thess. 3:2).

ἕνεκεν . . . . τοῦ εὐαγγελίου (Mark 8:35; 10:29).

κατὰ . . . . τὸ εὐαγγέλιον (Rom. 11:28; 16:25; I Tim. 1:11; II Tim. 2:8).
Without the article:

εἰς εὐαγγέλιον (Rom. 1:1; Gal. 1:6).

In Rom. 1:1 in the phrase ἀφωρισμένος εἰς εὐαγγέλιον θεοῦ there is a notable example of qualitative usage. There is, naturally, no indefiniteness, as if the apostle thought of God as the author of several gospels. Nor is there here any implicit contrast, as if there were, e.g., an εὐαγγέλιον θεοῦ and an εὐαγγέλιον διαβόλου or Σατανᾶ. It is not "a gospel of divine origin" that Paul has in mind, since he recognizes no other sort. Nor is it "the gospel of God," as if the article were prefixed according to his usual formula, though the definiteness of the reference is undeniable, nor "God's gospel," as εὐαγγέλιον θεοῦ might literally be rendered. Paul declares himself set apart to "good news" simply, with θεοῦ added as a qualifying nominal adjective. He is, then, "separated unto divine good news." The distinction between εὐαγγέλιον here and the prevailing τὸ εὐαγγέλιον elsewhere is quite as clear as that between "ministry" and "the ministry" or "service" and "the service." Obviously one might be spoken of as ordained to "ministry" who remained a layman, or as faithful in "service" who had no connection with any department of the state.

In Gal. 1:6 the term occurs in the prepositional phrase εἰς ἕτερον εὐαγγέλιον. That εὐαγγέλιον is not thought of indefinitely is shown by the immediately following words, ὃ οὐκ ἔστιν ἄλλο. To Paul there is only one "gospel," though that gospel may be perverted and presented in a debased form. The term cannot be indefinite because there is no class "gospels" in Paul's mind of which it can be a member. It is therefore qualitative.

3. *Qualitative usage other than in prepositional phrases.*—In one passage anarthrous εὐαγγέλιον occurs in an independent construction, viz., II Cor. 11:4. Here by the same argument adduced in the case of Gal. 1:6 it is shown to be qualitative. The fact that the apostle sets up no class "gospels" of which the εὐαγγέλιον ἕτερον can be a member shows that he uses the word qualitatively.

4. *The Revised Version renderings of* εὐαγγέλιον.—The Revised Version rendering of qualitative εὐαγγέλιον in Rom. 1:1, "separated unto the gospel of God," ignores the qualitative force of εὐαγγέλιον and renders it as if it were the customary τὸ εὐαγγέλιον. In II Cor. 11:4 and Gal. 1:6 the rendering "a different gospel," though it may imply an indefiniteness which was not present to Paul's mind, is perhaps as close an approach to the qualitative force of the Greek as is possible in English.

Θέλημα

1. *Statistical and comparative statement of usage.*—This term occurs 24 times in the Pauline Epistles, being in 13 instances restrictive and in 11 instances qualitative. There are some evidences that this word was employed without the article as a cult term for that which was conceived of as divinely preordained or less strictly for the divine desire. The passages in which such a meaning is apparent are Matt. 18:14; I Cor. 16:12. Others less convincing are I Thess. 4:3; 5:18; I Pet. 4:2. Apparently the early Christians could speak of what they regarded as divinely willed not only as "the will of God" (Rom. 12:2) or "God's will" (I Thess. 5:18) or "the will" (Rom. 2:18), but even more simply,

as "will" (I Cor. 16:12), and predicate that this or that was not θέλημα, meaning thereby that it was not divinely purposed (and therefore did not come to pass). Parallels are to be found in English in the usage of such words as "destiny," "providence," "kismet," "fate," "taboo," in anarthrous construction.

2. *Usage in prepositional phrases.*—The prepositional usage of θέλημα in the whole New Testament is as follows:

With the article:

ἐν τῷ θελήματι τοῦ θεοῦ (Rom. 1:10).

κατὰ τὸ θέλημα τοῦ θεοῦ (Gal. 1:4; I Pet. 4:19).

Without the article:

διὰ θελήματος θεοῦ (Rom. 15:32; I Cor. 1:1; II Cor. 1:1; 8:5; Eph. 1:1; Col. 1:1; II Tim. 1:1).

ἐν θελήματι τοῦ θεοῦ (Col. 4:12).

The foregoing data show that the use of διά with θέλημα is in the New Testament limited to Paul, that in this construction he always omits the article, though he employs it with ἐν in Rom. 1:10 and with κατά in Gal. 1:4. In all the instances of θέλημα with διά the noun is qualitative, as it is also with ἐν in Col. 4:12.

3. *Qualitative usage other than in prepositional phrases.*—Aside from prepositional constructions 3 instances of anarthrous θέλημα occur. Each may be quoted and discussed:

I Cor. 16:12: Περὶ δὲ Ἀπολλὼ τοῦ ἀδελφοῦ, πολλὰ παρεκάλεσα αὐτὸν ἵνα ἔλθῃ πρὸς ὑμᾶς μετὰ τῶν ἀδελφῶν· καὶ πάντως οὐκ ἦν θέλημα ἵνα νῦν ἔλθῃ, ἐλεύσεται δὲ ὅταν εὐκαιρήσῃ. "But as touching Apollos the brother, I besought him much to come unto you with the brethren: and it was not at all God's will that he should come now [margin]; but he will come when he shall have opportunity." This is a striking instance of the peculiar usage of θέλημα above referred to (a parallel occurs in Matt. 18:14). Apollos delays his journey, awaiting the time when the divine will shall be propitious. For him to depart to Corinth at the time of Paul's writing has in some way been determined to be not θέλημα, that is, divinely willed.

I Thess. 4:3: Τοῦτο γάρ ἐστιν θέλημα τοῦ θεοῦ . . . . ἀπέχεσθαι ὑμᾶς ἀπὸ τῆς πορνείας. "This is the will of God . . . . that ye abstain from fornication."

Also I Thess. 5:18: τοῦτο γὰρ θέλημα θεοῦ ἐν Χριστῷ Ἰησοῦ εἰς ὑμᾶς. "For this is the will of God in Christ Jesus to youward."

As in the first instance a given event was recognized not to be at a given time divinely willed, in the latter two a given course of action is declared θέλημα, i.e., a thing which God wills.   In the first the connotation of the term is evidently such that when used alone it carries a significance equivalent to that which it bears when used, as in the other two instances, with a qualifying τοῦ θεοῦ.   In all three the qualitative sense is pronounced.

4. *The Revised Version renderings of θέλημα.*—In I Cor. 16:12 the Revised Version refers the term to Apollos and translates: "It was not at all his will," with "God's will" as an alternative reading in the margin.   Here the marginal paraphrase is obviously the truer rendering, approximating the sense of the Greek, while not precisely representing its usage.

In I Thess. 4:3 and 5:18 the revisers have inserted the definite article, translating "the will of God," a rendering which, while correctly representing the definite reference of the phrase, makes the qualitative sense of "will" discoverable only by a consultation of the Greek.

Ἅγιος

1. *Statistical and comparative statement of usage.*—As a designation for Christians this term occurs 40 times in the Pauline writings, commonly in the plural, there being only 1 instance of its use in the singular (Phil. 4:21).   In the 27 occurrences in independent constructions it is used 22 times with and 5 times (Rom. 1:7; I Cor. 1:2; Eph. 3:8; 5:3; I Tim. 5:10) without the article.   In the 13 occurrences of the word in prepositional phrases only once (Rom. 8:27) is it anarthrous.

2. *Usage in prepositional phrases.*—A full exhibit of the prepositional usage of this term used as an appellative is as follows:
With the article:
εἰς τοὺς ἁγίους (I Cor. 16:1; II Cor. 8:4; 9:1; Eph. 1:15; Col. 1:4; Philem. 5).

ἐν τοῖς ἁγίοις (Eph. 1:18; II Thess. 1:10).

ἐπὶ τῶν ἁγίων (I Cor. 6:1).

μετὰ τῶν ἁγίων (I Thess. 3:13).

περὶ τῶν ἁγίων (Eph. 6:18).

σὺν τοῖς ἁγίοις (Eph. 3:18).
Without the article:
ὑπὲρ ἁγίων (Rom. 8:27).

Inasmuch as the only instance of anarthrous ἅγιος in a prepositional phrase is in Rom. 8:27, where the reference may be to things holy (cf. Matt. 7:6) rather than to Christians as such, the evidence for the qualitative usage of the term in prepositional phrases is indecisive.

54

3. *Qualitative usage other than in prepositional phrases.*—The 5 instances of anarthrous ἅγιος cited above are sufficient to show that while not common the usage of the term in a qualitative sense is definitely present in the Pauline Epistles. In 2 cases (Eph. 3:8 and I Tim. 5:10) the usage is indefinite, in the other 3 clearly qualitative. The 3 may be quoted and discussed: Rom. 1:7: πᾶσιν τοῖς οὖσιν ἐν Ῥώμῃ ἀγαπητοῖς θεοῦ, κλητοῖς ἁγίοις. I Cor. 1:1-2 is similar: Παῦλος . . . . τῇ ἐκκλησίᾳ . . . . ἐν Κορίνθῳ, ἡγιασμένοις ἐν Χριστῷ Ἰησοῦ, κλητοῖς ἁγίοις. Eph. 5:3: μηδὲ ὀνομαζέσθω ἐν ὑμῖν, καθὼς πρέπει ἁγίοις. In all 3 of these instances the omission of the article signifies the author's intention to emphasize the quality of saintliness, regarded as the peculiar property of Christians. They are, as we should say by italicization, *saints.* Holiness is regarded as the Christian's distinguishing mark, and to be holy is his appointed task. It is to the specific character of life to which they have been called that the apostle in the first 2 instances directs attention by the omission of the article. In Eph. 5:3 the term is likewise strictly qualitative. To saints sinful behavior is incongruous, that is, it is incompatible with the distinguishing Christian quality of saintliness.

4. *The Revised Version renderings of* ἅγιος.—In I Tim. 5:10 the insertion of the article before the indefinite ἁγίων is unwarranted. In Rom. 8:27, κατὰ θεὸν ἐντυγχάνει ὑπὲρ ἁγίων, where, even with the customary understanding of the term, the usage of ἁγίοις is clearly qualitative, the insertion of the definite article in the Revised Version fails in faithfulness to the Greek.

In the other instances in which ἁγίοις is clearly qualitative, the Revised Version translates by an anarthrous English equivalent and the qualitative effect is preserved.

Ἀδελφός

1. *Statistical and comparative statement of usage.*—In the Pauline Epistles ἀδελφός often occurs in the vocative plural in affectionate or expostulatory address.[1] In 2 instances the singular is so used (Philem. 7, 20). Very frequently the plural with the article is so used as a designation for the Christians of a given place. In Rom. 9:3 it is used to denote the Jewish nation. It is sometimes used indefinitely, as in I Cor. 7:12. In Rom. 14:10, 13, 15, 21 there are examples of ἀδελφός used generically. In I Cor. 9:5 it is used in its literal sense. A few instances of the qualitative usage occur.

---

[1] Such instances have been reckoned as qualitative.

2. *Usage in prepositional phrases.*—The following is an exhibit of the usage of ἀδελφός in prepositional phrases in the Pauline Epistles: With the article:

ἀνὰ μέσον τοῦ ἀδελφοῦ (I Cor. 6:5).

εἰς τοὺς ἀδελφούς (I Cor. 8:12; I Thess. 4:10).

ἐν τῷ ἀδελφῷ (I Cor. 7:14).

μετὰ τῶν ἀδελφῶν (I Cor. 16:11, 12).

σὺν Ὀνησίμῳ . . . . ἀδελφῷ (Col. 4:9).

ὑπὲρ τῶν ἀδελφῶν (Rom. 9:3).

Without the article:

ἀπὸ παντὸς ἀδελφοῦ (II Thess. 3:6).

ἐν πολλοῖς ἀδελφοῖς (Rom. 8:29).

In 8 cases ἀδελφός occurs with the article in prepositional phrases. In 6 of these it is used restrictively; in I Cor. 6:5 and 7:14 it is used generically. Anarthrous ἀδελφός occurs twice in prepositional phrases, being used once indefinitely and once in what is possibly a qualitative sense, viz., Rom. 8:29: ὅτι οὓς προέγνω, καὶ προώρισεν συμμόρφους τῆς εἰκόνος τοῦ υἱοῦ αὐτοῦ, εἰς τὸ εἶναι αὐτὸν πρωτότοκον ἐν πολλοῖς ἀδελφοῖς. "For whom he foreknew, he also foreordained to be conformed to the image of his Son, that he might be the first-born among many brethren." Here is an example of the indefinite and qualitative occasionally so shading into each other that it is difficult to say which usage was in the writer's mind.

3. *Qualitative usage other than in prepositional phrases.*—Ἀδελφός occurs occasionally in a distinctly qualitative sense. The following passage are examples:

I Cor. 5:11: νῦν δὲ ἔγραψα ὑμῖν . . . . ἐάν τις ἀδελφὸς ὀνομαζόμενος ᾖ πόρνος . . . . τῷ τοιούτῳ μηδὲ συνεσθίειν. "Now I write [margin] unto you, ... if any man that is named a brother be a fornicator, ... with such a one no, not to eat."

I Cor. 6:6: ἀλλὰ ἀδελφὸς μετὰ ἀδελφοῦ κρίνεται. "But brother goeth to law with brother."

I Cor. 6:8 is an especially noteworthy example of qualitative usage: ἀλλὰ ὑμεῖς ἀδικεῖτε καὶ ἀποστερεῖτε, καὶ τοῦτο ἀδελφούς. "Nay, but ye yourselves wrong and defraud, and that your *brethren.*"

I Tim. 5:1: ἀλλὰ παρακάλει . . . . νεωτέρους ὡς ἀδελφούς. "But exhort . . . . the younger men as brethren."

4. *The Revised Version renderings of* ἀδελφός.—In 3 of the foregoing instances of qualitative usage (viz., Rom. 8:29; I Cor. 6:6; I Tim. 5:1) the renderings of the Revised Version faithfully reflect the Greek. In

2 passages (I Cor. 5:11; 6:8) the translation is such as to obscure the qualitative force of the original. By the insertion of "a" before "brother" in I Cor. 5:11 the qualitative intention is impaired and the force of the sentence weakened. The person present to the apostle's mind is thought of not merely as "a brother," that is, a fellow-member of the Christian society, but as one who bears the Christian appellative "brother." The difference is one of emphasis. The offender is in either case within the Christian circle, but the apostle chooses to refer to him as one who bears the title "brother."

Similarly in I Cor. 6:8 the insertion of the pronoun "your" before "brethren" detracts from the force of the apostle's indignant protest. To his mind the incongruity of dishonesty on the part of the Corinthian Christians is aggravated by the fact that the dishonesty is practiced against members of the Christian brotherhood. The insertion of the pronoun contributes to smoothness but weakens the qualitative force.

Κλητός

1. *Statistical and comparative statement of usage.*—This term occurs 11 times in the New Testament, 7 of the instances being in Paul. It is used both with and without the article. In Matt. 20:16 and 22:14, where it is used in a play on words with ἐκλεκτός, its meaning is quite different from that which it has elsewhere in the New Testament. Ordinarily the κλητοί are the Christians, thought of simply as the fortunate objects of the divine invitation to become partakers of salvation, or with respect to some moral implication of their calling, or, in the case of Paul himself, with regard to his divine appointment to apostleship. Though the word may in every instance be regarded as an adjective, and is apparently so regarded by Thayer *et al.*, it seems possible that in some passages at least it is an adjective used as a noun and with a qualitative color. In Jude 1 and Rev. 17:14, indeed, the article appears and the nominal force is evident. The present writer ventures the hypothesis that κλητός was a cult term in use among the Christians and designated one as a member of the cult, quite as ἅγιος and ἀδελφός did. It may have been imported from the terminology of the Greek mysteries.

2. *Usage in prepositional phrases.*—No instances of prepositional usage occur.

3. *Qualitative usage other than in prepositional phrases.*—The following is the only clear example of the qualitative usage of κλητός: Rom 1:6: ἐστὲ καὶ ὑμεῖς κλητοὶ Ἰησοῦ Χριστοῦ. Here, while the apostle directs his readers' attention to the fact that they belong to a class, his intention

is evidently not to lay stress on membership in the class but upon the nature of the relationship thereby established. Still less do they constitute the class; they are not, then, thought of as "the called of Jesus Christ" but rather "called men of Jesus Christ" or "Jesus Christ's called."

4. *The Revised Version renderings of* κλητός.—In the instance just discussed the Revised Version takes κλητός in its usual verbal sense and reads "called to be Jesus Christ's," a rendering in which, while the qualitative intention is not wholly obscured, the emphasis is transferred to the title Ἰησοῦ Χριστοῦ, which is made predicative and telic instead of possessive.

Ἀπόστολος

1. *Statistical and comparative statement of usage.*—Out of a total of 34 occurrences in the Pauline Epistles 12 are instances of the restrictive usage, one (II Cor. 12:12) of the generic, and 21 of the qualitative. In 2 cases (II Cor. 8:23; Phil. 2:25) ἀπόστολος is used in its ordinary, non-official sense, "messenger."

2. *Usage in prepositional phrases.*—Ἀπόστολος occurs twice after a preposition, in both cases with the article and in the restrictive sense, viz., ἐν τοῖς ἀποστόλοις (Rom. 16:7); πρὸς τοὺς ἀποστόλους (Gal. 1:17).

3. *Qualitative usage other than in prepositional phrases.*—In 9 of the 13 epistles the address contains a reference to Paul as ἀπόστολος. In II Cor., Gal., Eph., Col., I Tim. and II Tim., and Titus the abrupt and strikingly qualitative Παῦλος ἀπόστολος is used. In Rom. 1:1 and I Cor. 1:1 the distinctively Pauline phrase κλητὸς ἀπόστολος is used. Upon the hypothesis that is put forward under the discussion of κλητός the conjunction of the two words may designate Paul as first a member of the Christian cult and secondly as occupying the position therein which the appellative ἀπόστολος was understood to denote.[1]

There remain 12 other instances of ἀπόστολος used qualitatively, the more outstanding of which may be discussed:

Rom. 11:13: εἰμὶ ἐγὼ ἐθνῶν ἀπόστολος. "I am an apostle of Gentiles." In this passage both nouns are qualitative, the emphasis lying upon ἐθνῶν. Paul affirms that to him belongs apostleship, and that of a specific character. An English rendering which exactly equates the Greek is "I am apostle of Gentiles." While the term ἀπόστολος is obviously restrictive, designating him as member of a class, the force of the term here is primarily qualitative, emphasizing the apostolic character of his relationship to the Gentiles.

---

[1] For a discussion of this term see Professor Ernest D. Burton, "The Office of Apostle in the Early Church," *American Journal of Theology*, October, 1912, pp. 561–88.

I Cor. 9:1: οὐκ εἰμὶ ἀπόστολος; "Am I not an apostle?" Here again Paul lays emphasis upon the character of his office as consonant with freedom in personal action and relationships, while at the same time indicating the class to which he belongs.

I Cor. 9:2: εἰ ἄλλοις οὐκ εἰμὶ ἀπόστολος, ἀλλά γε ὑμῖν εἰμί. "If to others I am not an apostle, yet at least I am to you." From the context the purport of this statement appears to be that while others may repudiate his claim to apostleship he may expect the Corinthians to recognize its validity. The qualitative force may be brought out in English by printing the word with quotation marks: "If to others I am not 'apostle' I am at least to you."

I Cor. 15:9: Ἐγὼ γάρ εἰμι ὁ ἐλάχιστος τῶν ἀποστόλων, ὃς οὐκ εἰμὶ ἱκανὸς καλεῖσθαι ἀπόστολος. "For I am the least of the apostles, that am not meet to be called an apostle." Here again the term is qualitative, Paul expressing his feeling that his previous persecution of the Christians made him unfit to receive from them subsequently the honorable title "apostle."

4. *The Revised Version renderings of ἀπόστολος.*—The Revised Version habitually translates ἀπόστολος with the indefinite article, a practice which, though weakening the qualitative effect, is in keeping with English idiom. Rom. 11:13 is a typical example. The qualitative force of ἐθνῶν remains unimpaired in the translation, but ἀπόστολος is stripped of its qualitative character, the modifying phrase "of Gentiles" contributing to this effect. In English it is common to prefix the indefinite article to a noun used qualitatively when the noun stands alone (see p. 8). When, however, a modifying phrase is added as here, and in translation the passage is made to read "an apostle of Gentiles," the qualitative character of the appellative disappears and it becomes merely a class designation. Apart from reference to the underlying Greek the reader of the English text is not made aware of the qualitative character of ἀπόστολος as he is of ἐθνῶν. In all the epistolary addresses where anarthrous ἀπόστολος occurs the bold qualitative is similarly reduced by the prefixing of the indefinite article. In 4 passages (I Cor. 12:28, 29; II Cor. 11:13; I Thess. 2:6) ἀπόστολος is rendered by its anarthrous English equivalent and the qualitative force is thereby adequately expressed.

Ἐπίσκοπος

1. *Statistical and comparative statement of usage.*—The infrequency of this term in the New Testament, even in its later portions, is in striking contrast to its prominence in subsequent church history. It occurs

5 times in the whole New Testament, 3 times in the Pauline Epistles. In Phil. 1:1 it is the object of a preposition. In both the other instances (I Tim. 3:2; Titus 1:7) the article precedes and the noun is generic.

2. *Usage in prepositional phrases.*—Two instances of ἐπίσκοπος in prepositional phrases occur in the New Testament, viz., with the article, ἐπὶ τὸν . . . . ἐπίσκοπον (I Pet. 2:25); without the article, σὺν ἐπισκόποις (Phil. 1:1). In Phil. 1:1 the apostle addresses the saints at Philippi σὺν ἐπισκόποις καὶ διακόνοις. Both nouns are used qualitatively and may be represented in English by the rendering "bishops and deacons included."

3. *Qualitative usage other than in prepositional phrases.*—No instance of such usage occurs.

4. *The Revised Version renderings of* ἐπίσκοπος.—In the Philippians passage the Revised Version inserts the article, perhaps assuming that the definitive force of the article in τοῖς ἁγίοις and τοῖς οὖσιν carries over to the prepositional phrase or else feeling that smoothness of translation requires its presence. Thereby also the ambiguity to which a literal translation would be subject (as if the apostle were limiting his address to those Philippian Christians who possessed these officers) is avoided. Nevertheless the careful New Testament student is in duty bound to observe the absence of the article at this point and to consider whether its presence in the English translation is justified.

Σωτήρ

1. *Statistical and comparative statement of usage.*—As a common term in the cult of the emperor[1] this word acquires a significance and interest out of proportion to the frequency of its occurrence in the New Testament. It occurs not infrequently in the LXX and is applied both to God and men, designating in the latter case those judges who rescued Israel from oppression (Judg. 3:9, 13; Neh. 12:3). In the New Testament it is applied only to God and Jesus Christ. Its precise significance in the New Testament is a topic for an investigation of a different nature from the one in hand and has been treated at length by several authorities.[2] Σωτήρ occurs in the whole New Testament 24 times. In 8 of these it is coupled with θεός as a title for God. In all other instances

---

[1] See Case, *Evolution of Early Christianity*, chapter vii, "The Religious Significance of Emperor Worship" and literature there cited, especially Heinen, *Zur Begründung des römischen Kaiserkultus: chronologische Übersicht von 43 v. bis 14 n. Chr.;* also H. F. Burton, "The Worship of the Roman Emperors," *Biblical World*, August, 1912, pp. 80–91.

[2] E.g., Paul Wendland, *ZNTW*, V (1904), 335 ff.

it is applied to Jesus, usually with concomitant terms (i.e., κύριος [II Pet. 3:18]; υἱός [I John 4:14]; Ἰησοῦς Χριστός [II Tim. 1:10]) and commonly with the article. It occurs with comparative infrequency in the Pauline literature, being found only twice (Eph. 5:23; Phil. 3:20) outside the Pastoral Epistles. In these it occurs 10 times, in 6 being applied to God and in 4 to Jesus. Its importance as bearing upon the authorship of the Pastoral Epistles is obvious.

2. *Usage in prepositional phrases.*—The usage in the whole New Testament is as follows:

With the article:

ἀπὸ .... τοῦ σωτῆρος (Titus 1:4).
διὰ .... τοῦ σωτῆρος (Titus 3:6).
ἐνώπιον τοῦ σωτῆρος (I Tim. 2:3).
ἐπὶ τῷ σωτῆρι (Luke 1:47).

No instance of anarthrous σωτήρ in a prepositional phrase occurs.

3. *Qualitative usage other than in prepositional phrases.*—There are 3 instances of qualitative σωτήρ in the Pauline Epistles, the Pastorals being included, as follows:

Eph. 5:23: καὶ ὁ χριστὸς κεφαλὴ τῆς ἐκκλησίας, αὐτὸς σωτὴρ τοῦ σώματος. "As Christ also is the head of the church, being himself the saviour of the body."[1]

I Tim. 1:1: Παῦλος ἀπόστολος Χριστοῦ Ἰησοῦ κατ' ἐπιταγὴν θεοῦ σωτῆρος ἡμῶν. "Paul, an apostle of Christ Jesus according to the commandment of God our Saviour."[2]

I Tim. 4:10: ὅς ἐστιν σωτὴρ πάντων ἀνθρώπων, μάλιστα πιστῶν. "Who is the Saviour of all men, specially of them that believe."

In each of the foregoing instances of anarthrous σωτήρ its reference is definite, but it is used qualitatively to ascribe the intrinsic characteristic of saviourhood to God or to Christ, rather than to designate either restrictively as "the Saviour."

4. *The Revised Version renderings of σωτήρ.*—In Eph. 5:23 the Revised Version wrongly translates θεός with the definite article, thus affording one of those instances, comparatively rare, where an anarthrous Greek noun is rendered in English by a noun preceded by the definite article. In the rendering of I Tim. 4:10 occurs another instance of the insertion of the definite article in translation before a noun anarthrous in the Greek. This sharpening of the qualitative into the

---

[1] Note the mistranslation of the qualitative κεφαλή, properly rendered in Eph. 1:22.

[2] Note also the mistranslation of κατ' ἐπιταγήν. Cf. also Rom. 16:26; Titus 1:3. It is correctly rendered in I Cor. 7:6; II Cor. 8:8.

restrictive usage is without justification. In Phil. 3:20, where σωτήρ is probably indefinite, the Revised Version appropriately translates "a Saviour."

Κύριος

1. *Statistical and comparative statement of usage.*—Next to θεός this appellative is probably the most frequent in the New Testament, occurring 725 times, 280 of these being in Paul.[1] It is used both with and without the article. The prevailing usage is to employ the article, but in 108 instances κύριος is anarthrous. Sixteen of these are in Old Testament quotations, where the reference is to God; 64 are in prepositional phrases; 28 are in independent constructions other than in passages quoted from the Old Testament. In nearly all these last κύριος is used qualitatively, but see I Cor. 8:5, where it is used indefinitely.

2. *Usage in prepositional phrases.*—Κύριος occurs frequently in prepositional phrases and with striking preference for the anarthrous form. Of the 64 occurrences in prepositional phrases only 6 are preceded by the article. More than half, then, of the instances of anarthrous κύριος are in prepositional phrases, and in prepositional phrases κύριος is in 90 per cent of the instances anarthrous. A full exhibition of the Pauline prepositional usage of κύριος is as follows:

With the article:

ἀπὸ τοῦ κυρίου (I Cor. 11:23).

διὰ τοῦ κυρίου (Rom. 5:1, 11; 15:30; I Thess. 4:2; 5:9).

Without the article:

ἀπὸ κυρίου (Rom. 1:7; I Cor. 1:3; II Cor. 1:2; 3:18; Gal. 1:3; Eph. 1:2; 6:23; Phil. 1:2; Col. 3:24; II Thess. 1:1; Philem. 3).

ἐν κυρίῳ (Rom. 14:14; 16:2, 8, 11, 12 [*bis*], 13, 22; I Cor. 1:31; 4:17; 7:22, 39; 9:1, 2; 11:11; 15:58; 16:19; II Cor. 2:12; 10:17; Eph. 2:21; 4:1, 17; 5:8; 6:1, 10, 21; Phil. 1:14; 2:19, 24, 29; 3:1; 4:1, 2, 4, 10; Col. 3:18, 20; 4:7, 17; I Thess. 1:1; 3:8; 4:1; 5:12; II Thess. 3:4, 12; Philem. 16, 20).

ἐνώπιον κυρίου (II Cor. 8:21).

ἐπὶ κύριον (I Tim. 5:5 [margin]).

παρὰ κυρίου (Eph. 6:8).

πρὸς κύριον (II Cor. 3:16).

σὺν κυρίῳ (I Thess. 4:17).

ὑπὸ κυρίου (I Cor. 7:25; II Thess. 2:13).

[1] It is noteworthy that of the 280 instances in Paul only 7 are used in a sense other than as referring to God or to Christ, viz., Rom. 14:4; I Cor. 8:5; Gal. 1:4; Eph. 6:5, 9; Col. 3:22; 4:1.

Of the 6 instances where κύριος with the article is the object of a preposition the latter is never ἐν and the relation is measurably, at least, objective, and the person referred to individualized. In actual usage ἐν κυρίῳ, occurring 46 times, expresses not a spatial idea, though the spatial conception is doubtless the basis of the phrase, but the spiritual, mystical relationship of the Christian to the heavenly Christ, which in turn entails various spiritual benefits and imposes various duties. It is to be noted that no instance of ἐν τῷ κυρίῳ occurs, a fact which argues for the hypothesis here put forward, namely, that in the prepositional phrase ἐν κυρίῳ the noun is not to be regarded as definite, although the revisers have invariably so translated it, but as qualitative, being used as a technical term, expressive of the mystical relationship of the believer to Christ or a cult designation for the circle of Christian fellowship. The qualitative character of the phrase is apparently reflected in the omission of the article before the noun.

The evidence of the prepositional usage examined in this investigation tends to establish the principle that in Paul, at least, nouns in prepositional phrases are anarthrous when the prepositional phrase itself is qualitative. In such cases the noun itself may not strictly be regarded as qualitative though the phrase is. The qualitative character of the phrase is indicated by the omission of the article before the noun, since there is no article before the phrase whose omission would indicate this character. The statement sometimes made that nouns in prepositional phrases tend to be anarthrous is true to this extent, that nouns in prepositional phrases are anarthrous when the phrase itself is qualitative. In general the omission of the article before nouns in prepositional phrases is clearly deliberate, with the intention of indicating their qualitative force. The noun after a preposition in no wise differs in its articular usage from a noun not used after a preposition (see, e.g., II Cor. 11:23, 26), but is anarthrous when indefinite or qualitative, or when the phrase itself is qualitative. In the case of ἐν κυρίῳ these points are illustrated. Κύριος is not indefinite and it is not itself qualitative. It is the whole phrase which is used qualitatively and therefore, though the reference is perfectly definite, the noun in the phrase is made anarthrous as an indication of the qualitative character of the phrase.

3. *Qualitative usage other than in prepositional phrases.*—There are 28 instances of κύριος used qualitatively in constructions other than prepositional phrases and in passages other than those quoted from the Old Testament. As typical instances may be cited Rom. 10:9: ἐὰν ὁμολογήσῃς . . . . ὅτι ΚΥΡΙΟΣ ΙΗΣΟΥΣ . . . . σωθήσῃ; also I Cor. 8:6:

[ἀλλ'] ἡμῖν . . . . καὶ εἷς κύριος Ἰησοῦς Χριστός. In these passages it is the lordship of Jesus which is demanded and asserted, the term κύριος being strongly qualitative. The remaining instances of this character are Rom. 14:6 (*ter*); I Cor. 4:4; 7:22, 25; 10:21 (*bis*); 12:3; 14:37; 16:10; II Cor. 4:5; 12:1; Gal. 4:1; Eph. 4:5; 6:4; Phil. 2:11, 30; 3:20; Col. 3:17; 4:1; I Thess. 4:6, 15; 5:2; I Tim. 6:15; II Tim. 2:24. In a few passages, of which Phil. 3:20 is an illustration, κύριος without the article occurs as a part of the title Κύριος Ἰησοῦς Χριστός, in which the 3 terms constitute a single proper name, but the qualitative character of the appellative is at the same time preserved, as in the English "Captain John Smith," "President Wilson," etc.

4. *The Revised Version renderings of* κύριος.—In its renderings of anarthrous κύριος the Revised Version has usually employed the definite article, ἐν κυρίῳ, for example, being usually rendered "in the Lord," which, however, was necessary inasmuch as English idiom does not permit the phrase "in Lord," though it does allow "in Christ" or "in God." In those passages in which the acknowledgment that Jesus is κύριος is set forth as the essential Christian creed (Rom. 10:9; I Cor. 12:3; Phil. 2:11; cf. II Cor. 4:5) the Revised Version preserves the qualitative effect by an anarthrous rendering. The expression of the qualitative character of κύριος in prepositional phrases may well be practically impossible in English and the renderings of the Revised Version, therefore, may be as exact an equivalent as is feasible. In general, then, the treatment accorded the term in the Revised Version is insusceptible to dissenting criticism.

Θεός

1. *Statistical and comparative statement of usage.*—As one of the most frequent appellatives, appearing 1,326 times in the whole New Testament and 520 times in Paul, this word is worthy of a detailed attention which its extraordinary frequency renders all the more difficult. Out of the 520 occurrences in Paul, 158 are clear instances of θεός without the article. Four others in the phrase τοῦ σωτῆρος ἡμῶν θεοῦ (I Tim. 2:3; Titus 1:3; 2:10; 3:4) are questionable. Of the 158, 41 are in prepositional phrases. In nearly all instances where anarthrous θεός occurs it is in the oblique cases, occurring chiefly as a genitive modifier, but a few occurrences of the nominative must be admitted, viz., Rom. 8:33; 9:5; I Cor. 8:4; Phil. 2:13; I Thess. 2:5; I Tim. 3:16; Titus 1:16.

2. *Usage in prepositional phrases.*—The prepositional usage of θεός in the whole New Testament is as follows:

With the article:

ἀπὸ τοῦ θεοῦ (Luke 1:26; Acts 2:22; 26:22; Rom. 15:15; Heb. 6:7; Rev. 3:12; 12:6; 20:9; 21:2, 10).

εἰς τὸν θεόν (John 14:1; Acts 6:11; 24:15).

ἐκ τοῦ θεοῦ (John 6:33; 7:17; 8:42, 47 [*bis*]; Rom. 2:29; I Cor. 2:12; 11:12; II Cor. 3:5; 5:18; I John 3:9 [*bis*], 10; 4:1, 2, 3, 4, 6 [*bis*], 7 [*bis*]; 5:1, 4, 18 [*bis*], 19; III John 11; Rev. 11:11).

ἔμπροσθεν τοῦ θεοῦ (Acts 10:4; I Cor. 4:5; I Thess. 3:9, 13).

ἐν τῷ θεῷ (Rom. 5:11; Eph. 3:9; Col. 3:3; I Thess. 2:2; I John 4:15, 16).

ἔναντι τοῦ θεοῦ (Luke 1:8; Acts 8:21).

ἐναντίον τοῦ θεοῦ (Luke 1:6; 24:19).

ἐνώπιον τοῦ θεοῦ (Luke 1:19; 12:6; 16:15; Acts 4:19; 7:46; 10:31, 33; Rom. 14:22; I Cor. 1:29; II Cor. 4:2; 7:12; Gal. 1:20; I Tim. 5:4, 21; 6:13; II Tim. 2:14; 4:1; Rev. 3:2; 8:2, 4; 9:13; 11:16; 12:10; 16:19).

ἐπὶ τῷ θεῷ (Luke 1:47; II Cor. 1:9).

ἐπὶ τὸν θεόν (Matt. 27:43; Acts 15:19; 26:18, 20; I Tim. 5:5).

κατὰ τοῦ θεοῦ (Matt. 26:63; I Cor. 15:15).

παρὰ τοῦ θεοῦ (John 5:44; 6:46; 8:40; 16:27).

παρὰ τῷ θεῷ (Mark 10:27; Luke 1:37; 18:27; Rom. 2:11, 13; 9:14; I Cor. 3:19; Gal. 3:11; Jas. 1:27).

πρὸς τὸν θεόν (John 1:1, 2; 13:3; 20:17; Acts 12:5; 24:16; Rom. 5:1; 10:1; 15:17, 30; II Cor. 3:4; 13:7; Phil. 4:6; I Thess. 1:8, 9; Heb. 2:17; 5:1; I John 3:21; Rev. 12:5; 13:6).

ὑπὸ τοῦ θεοῦ (Matt. 22:31; Acts 10:41; 26:6; I Cor. 2:12; II Cor. 1:4; Gal. 3:17; I Thess. 1:4; 2:4; Heb. 5:4, 10).

Without the article:

ἀπὸ θεοῦ (John 3:2; 13:3; 16:30; Rom. 1:7; I Cor. 1:3, 30; 6:19; II Cor. 1:2; Gal. 1:3; Eph. 1:2; 6:23; Phil. 1:2, 28; Col. 1:2; II Thess. 1:2; I Tim. 1:2; II Tim. 1:2; Titus 1:4; Philem. 3; Heb. 3:12; Jas. 1:13; II Pet. 1:21).

διὰ θεοῦ (Gal. 1:1; 4:7).

εἰς θεόν (Luke 12:21; Rom. 8:7; I Pet. 1:21; 3:5, 21).

ἐκ θεοῦ (John 1:13; Acts 5:39; I Cor. 7:7; II Cor. 2:17; 5:1; Phil. 3:9).

ἐν θεῷ (Rom. 2:17; I Thess. 1:1; II Thess. 1:1; Jude 1).

ἐπὶ θεῷ (I Tim. 4:10; 6:17).

ἐπὶ θεόν (Acts 14:15; Heb. 6:1).

κατὰ θεόν (Rom. 8:27; II Cor. 7:9, 10, 11; Eph. 4:24; I Pet. 4:6; 5:2).

κατέναντι θεοῦ (Rom. 4:17; II Cor. 12:19).

παρὰ θεοῦ (John 1:6; 9:33; II Pet. 1:17; II John 3).

παρὰ θεῷ (Matt. 19:26; Mark 10:27; Luke 2:52; I Cor. 7:24; II Thess. 1:6; I Pet. 2:4, 20).

πρὸς θεόν (Rom. 4:2).

ὑπὸ θεοῦ (Rom. 13:1 [*bis*]; Gal. 4:9).

The foregoing exhibit discloses the following facts: θεός with and without the article is used in prepositional phrases in the whole New Testament 199 times; in 67 instances it is anarthrous, in 132 articular. In Paul θεός occurs in prepositional phrases 86 times, 41 of which are anarthrous; in the Lucan writings 32 times, 4 of which are anarthrous; in the Johannine writings 55 times, 7 of which are anarthrous; in the Epistle to the Hebrews 7 times, 2 of which are anarthrous; in James twice, 1 of which is anarthrous; in I and II Peter 9 times, all of which are anarthrous. These data suggest that the New Testament usage of θεός in prepositional phrases is precisely that of nouns in other constructions, viz., the article is dropped or retained according to the idea the writer desires to convey. If in his thought the term is restrictive or generic he employs the article; if in his thought the term is indefinite or qualitative he omits the article as a sign of that fact. If he employs the prepositional phrase as a whole qualitatively he omits the article before the noun in the phrase to show that the phrase is so intended, though the noun itself may not be strictly qualitative and though its reference may be perfectly definite. In no single instance of the 67 cases of anarthrous θεός which the New Testament presents is the reference to any other than the Jewish and Christian deity, and in every case the absence of the article indicates either that the word θεός is used qualitatively or that the prepositional phrase as a whole is so used.

3. *Qualitative usage other than in prepositional phrases.*—In general θεός without the article is qualitative (adjectival), approximating the adjective θεῖος or the abstract noun θειότης (I Tim. 3:16). A few instances of θεός used qualitatively may be discussed, e.g.:

Rom. 1:17: δικαιοσύνη γὰρ θεοῦ ἐν αὐτῷ ἀποκαλύπτεται. "For therein [in the gospel] is revealed a righteousness of God."

Rom. 1:18: ἀποκαλύπτεται γὰρ ὀργὴ θεοῦ. "For the [margin "a"] wrath of God is revealed."

The "righteousness" and "wrath" are conceived of here as distinguished by the characteristics which God possesses. That which is revealed is "divine righteousness," "divine wrath." While the anarthrous noun refers as definitely to God as if the article were present, the omission of the article indicates that it is not God as the possessor or imposer of righteousness or wrath which is foremost in the apostle's thought, but the peculiar character which belongs to righteousness and wrath by virtue of the fact that they proceed from God.

Rom. 8:9: εἴπερ πνεῦμα θεοῦ οἰκεῖ ἐν ὑμῖν. "If so be that the spirit of God dwelleth in you."

Rom. 8:14: ὅσοι γὰρ πνεύματι θεοῦ ἄγονται, οὗτοι υἱοὶ θεοῦ εἰσίν. "But as many as are led by the spirit of God, these are sons of God."

In these instances πνεῦμα θεοῦ is to be distinguished from τὸ πνεῦμα τοῦ θεοῦ, not in respect to the definiteness of its reference but in respect to the emphasis laid upon the quality both of πνεῦμα and θεοῦ. In neither of the cases cited above is it "the spirit of God," thought of restrictively, but "divine spirit," thought of qualitatively; that is to say, one may conceive of a spiritual influence emanating from deity and denominate it "the spirit of God," that is, the certain spirit which God possesses or of which he is the source. Thinking of this same spirit qualitatively we may call it "divine spirit," that is to say, spirit whose characteristics are akin to or identical with those of deity itself. As a matter of fact the definitive content of the two expressions may be precisely identical; in the one case, however, the writer uses the expression restrictively, in the other qualitatively.

I Cor. 1:1: Παῦλος κλητὸς ἀπόστολος Ἰησοῦ Χριστοῦ διὰ θελήματος θεοῦ. "Paul called to be an apostle of Jesus Christ through the will of God."

*I Cor. 1:18: Ὁ λόγος γὰρ ὁ τοῦ σταυροῦ . . . . δύναμις θεοῦ ἐστίν. "For the word of the cross . . . . is the power of God."

Rom. 1:16: οὐ γὰρ ἐπαισχύνομαι τὸ εὐαγγέλιον, δύναμις γὰρ θεοῦ ἐστίν. "For I am not ashamed of the gospel: for it is the power of God."

In all the above θεός is used qualitatively. In I Cor. 1:1 Paul's apostleship is grounded upon divine intention. In this, as in all other occurrences of the Pauline phrase, διὰ θελήματος θεοῦ, the phrase is to be understood as equal to "by divine decree." In I Cor. 1:18 and Rom. 1:16 the gospel message is called "divine power." In Rom. 1:16 the gospel is not thought of (as the English translation would indicate) as that particular "power" belonging to God through which salvation is achieved, but simply as divine power working toward a definite end which is itself thought of qualitatively (σωτηρίαν not τὴν σωτηρίαν). It is, rendering the thought accurately, "divine power directed to the production of human salvation."

I Cor. 8:4: οἴδαμεν . . . . ὅτι οὐδεὶς θεὸς εἰ μὴ εἷς.　"We know . . . . that there is no God but one."

I Cor. 8:5: καὶ γὰρ εἴπερ εἰσὶν λεγόμενοι θεοὶ εἴτε ἐν οὐρανῷ εἴτε ἐπὶ γῆς, ὥσπερ εἰσὶν θεοὶ πολλοὶ καὶ κύριοι πολλοί, [ἀλλ'] ἡμῖν εἷς θεὸς ὁ πατήρ. "For though there be that are called gods, whether in heaven or on earth; as there are gods many, and lords many; yet to us there is one God, the Father."

Gal. 4:8: ἐδουλεύσατε τοῖς φύσει μὴ οὖσι θεοῖς.　"Ye were in bondage to them that by nature are no gods."

II Thess. 2:4: ὁ . . . . ὑπεραιρόμενος ἐπὶ πάντα λεγόμενον θεόν.　"He that exalteth himself against all that is called God."

In I Cor. 8:4, 6, where are found what are perhaps the clearest instances of the qualitative usage of θεός which the New Testament affords, the θεὸς ὁ πατήρ, who to Paul is the only being actually θεός, is contrasted with those whom he dismisses as merely θεοί so called.

In Gal. 4:8 the apostle denies the right of the gods previously worshiped by the Galatians to the title θεός.　The term is obviously strongly qualitative, the apostle's thought being that these previously worshiped gods were lacking in the characteristics which are proper to deity.

In II Thess. 2:4 also θεός is clearly qualitative, the quality foremost in the writer's thought being the right of a θεός to reverential treatment.

4. *The Revised Version renderings of* θεός.—The revisers' fixed rule has been to translate θεός literally.　Inasmuch as in English idiom the name of deity is regularly anarthrous this leaves the qualitative effect to be recognized only by reference to the Greek and to be expressed in English either by circumlocution or by mental or vocal emphasis.

Though to give accurate renderings of θεός used qualitatively would have increased the difficulty of the translators' work and have involved a greater degree of departure from the Authorized Version than the rules of the company contemplated, the English reader had the right to expect that such accurate renderings would be furnished.　A translator is under obligation to give his reader a version that shall be true both to the letter and the spirit of the original.　The mere substitution of the English term "God" for the Greek θεός fails to acquaint the reader with the qualitative intention of the author's usage.　If to discover this the reader must have recourse to the Greek the translation has obviously in so far failed to achieve the very purpose for which it was made.

IV. SUMMARY OF THE RESULTS OF THE STUDY

In the Greek text of the Pauline Epistles there occur 8,841 nouns and noun equivalents. Of these some 2,857 are used qualitatively. Of these 2,445 are so translated as to express in English the qualitative force of the original, while in 412 instances this has been obscured either by a failure to recognize the qualitative character of the noun in ques-' tion or by a failure adequately to express that character in English. In some of these cases doubtless an ambiguous rendering of the qualitative force of the Greek is impossible. In others, a reader, familiar with the Greek, and observing the qualitative character of the noun, may in reading give the proper emphasis either mentally or vocally, but he cannot discover it from the English. The difference between English and Greek idiom doubtless renders a translation that is at the same time accurate and idiomatic, difficult and sometimes impossible. At the same time the English reader has a right to expect from a translator that he will give him whenever possible such a rendering of qualitative nouns as shall enable him to recognize their qualitative character without the necessity of reference to the original, and this the revisers have in the majority of cases, but by no means uniformly, done.

The ascertainment of the relative correctness of the Revised Version in its renderings of qualitative nouns fulfils the secondary purpose of the investigation. The primary purpose was the discovery and listing of the nouns used qualitatively, together with such discussion as the limits of the dissertation allow, in the conviction that due attention to this element of New Testament lexicography will contribute to a more accurate interpretation of the New Testament.

Incidentally the investigation has shown that nouns after prepositions have no peculiar usage respecting the use of the article by virtue of that fact. Anarthrous nouns in prepositional phrases, like such nouns in other constructions, are in general either indefinite or qualitative. The general proposition that nouns in prepositional phrases are either indefinite or qualitative requires modification only to the extent that nouns in prepositional phrases themselves qualitative or formulary tend to omit the article even if the noun is not itself, strictly speaking, qualitative. The evidence indicates that Pauline usage is not lax but accurate, i.e., strictly in accordance with fixed principles. When the prepositional phrase is itself qualitative that qualitative character is shown by the omission of the article though the noun is not itself strictly qualitative. The failure to recognize this fact has led New Testament grammarians (e.g., Winer, Buttmann) into intricate and often erroneous observations.

www.ingramcontent.com/pod-product-compliance
Lightning Source LLC
Chambersburg PA
CBHW062026040426
42447CB00010B/2156